Money
Handbook

Spiritual Keys and Practical Steps to Finance

Samia Pedalino

ISBN: 9780578924250 (Paperback)

Library of Congress Control Number: 2021902580

Front cover image by Leilani Hayes.

Printed by KDP amazon, in the United States of America.

First printing edition 2021.

"I will place on his shoulder the key to the house of David; what he opens no one can shut, and what he shuts no one can open."

Isaiah 22:22

Meet the Author

Samia is an entrepreneur, author, and communicator with a passion to help you learn how to manage money, build wealth, and connect your faith to your finances. Raised in a traditional Jewish home in sunny South Florida, she carries a deep value for stewarding kingdom finances. With years of experience as a financial advisor and later as a successful business owner, Samia shares her wisdom and knowledge from both a biblical and practical perspective.

When Samia is not chasing her toddlers around, she has a strong appreciation for a really good glass of wine and a great charcuterie board.

Samia holds a BSBA in Marketing from University of Florida's Warrington College of Business. She resides in Redding, CA with her husband Nicholas and their two children, Noah and Ariyel.

Contact: SamiaPedalino.com

Connect on Instagram: @moneyhandbook

Acknowledgments

Thank you to my husband Nicholas who told me in the first year of our marriage, in 2015, I would write a book on finance and have a platform to encourage women to live their fullest as daughters of the King. At the time, I thought it was very sweet of him to believe in me and to think I had wisdom others would benefit from. His words of discernment and insight have certainly come full circle. He is the pillar of our family and this book would not have happened without his support and of course, baby duty while I snuck away to write!

Thank you to my parents. Mom, you gave me a solid scriptural foundation and instilled in me a royal identity while modeling what a true believer in Yeshua is. Dad, your vigilance has saved me from countless bad decisions and your ability to financially provide is a direct result of my firmly rooted belief, that God is my Provider.

Thank you to my friend and editor Tiffany Lovett. Your deep well of knowledge and incredible feedback helped shape the message of this book. You pushed me forward and helped to draw out twenty years of experience! I will be forever grateful for your time and dedication on this project.

To all the family members, friends, and acquaintances who have cheered me on, purchased the book and told others about it, thank you! Your stories have inspired me and you have been a beautiful example of what a supportive and loving community is all about.

Table of Contents

Welcome

Welcome to the Money Handbook, spiritual keys and practical steps to finance. I wrote this book to share with you the wisdom I gained through my experience in finance, both as a business owner and growing up in a traditional Jewish home. To the best of my ability, I present you with the spiritual truths of God's heart for money and its purpose in your life. I give biblical examples and practical steps to empower you, so you can implement a financial plan for your family.

In this book, you will find chapters focused on giving, saving, investing, insurance, and raising children, all of which will equip you with financial strategy. I hope the knowledge and spiritual keys shared in each chapter help you tend to the soil of your specific situation so you can reap a great harvest in your life.

In closing, one of my favorite prayers is the priestly blessing God told Moses to have his brother Aaron speak over the Israelites. In three short sentences God covers so much! Blessings, protection, grace, favor, and peace which can only come from the Lord. My prayer for you today is for God to bless you and protect you. To make His face shine upon you and be gracious to you. And, for God to look upon you with favor and give you His Peace (Numbers 6:22-27). May the Lord increase you a thousand times and bless you as He has promised.

Let's get started, I'm so glad you are here!
Samia

Chapter One

Money Mindsets

B efore writing this book, I sent out a questionnaire to friends in the United States, the United Kingdom, and Israel. They all come from different financial and denominational backgrounds but have one fact in common; their faith in Jesus. Some of them grew up with money and others were raised with none. Some were educated on basic financial lessons while others were taught nothing. One of the questions I asked them was, "What are your first thoughts when you think of the word money?" I specifically asked this to find out the different mindsets people learned from their upbringing. The most common answers were; money equates to sin, it is evil in nature, or not something to be desired. The majority of the answers also stated money was never spoken about or taught in their home or school. And, if it was mentioned in their church, only tithing was discussed. This was a sad reality for me to discover and the overwhelming reason why I wrote this book. There is a popular saying, "Knowledge is power," and I believe it applies to finance because gaining knowledge and having a good understanding of money will empower you to make wise choices.

Thousand Dollar Check

Imagine you are in the grocery store and someone walks up to you and says, "God led me to give you this check and I hope it blesses you." Then, the person walks away before you can refuse it. Standing there in a bit of disbelief you open the check and it is written out for $1,000! All you have to do is write in your name on the top line of the check. What is your first thought?

1. Guilt and Shame: "I can't accept this because I didn't do anything to deserve it, I am not worthy of this gift."
2. Poverty: "I am not telling anyone about this, I am going to hoard it."
3. Joy and Freedom: "Thank you sweet Jesus, I knew you would meet my needs, who can I bless this week?"

Your answer to the $1,000 check question, whatever it may be, will tell you more about your mindsets regarding money than what's in your bank account. What are your first thoughts when you hear the word money? Everyone has beliefs associated with it and what you think or believe to be true will affect the financial decisions you make in life. Do you feel fear, insecurity, disgust, or inadequate? If you answered yes, then my goal for you is to finish this book with confidence and trust in your ability to steward money well and begin to build wealth.

The Recipe

My husband is a much better cook than me, and I think most of you reading this, has a meal that is easy for you to make and always a huge hit when you serve it. If I were to ask my husband how to prepare his famous meatballs, it would not be difficult for him to explain the cooking directions to me since he has experience making it. He would probably send me the recipe by text, including the list of items to buy along with exact cooking directions. Money works the same way. Similar to a recipe, it is like the practice of consistently combining multiple ingredients which result in a delicious meal that blesses not only you, but your family and friends too.

Some of those ingredients are the mindsets and habits you have towards money, giving, saving, and the use of debt. If one ingredient is out of balance, it will change the outcome of the meal and potentially make it inedible. Family upbringing, people followed on social media, movies and tv shows, and the friends in your inner circle can influence your opinion about money. Think about what your parents said or did not say about money during your childhood. Think about the tv shows you watched growing up and the values they taught you about money. Reflect on the impact social media influencers have in your life regarding your opinion of money. Whether you are fully aware of it or not, all the things mentioned above will have an effect on your money mindset. But what if your mindset about your finances was only influenced by the things God has to say? It might look different from the ideas you were raised to believe, but who wants a counterfeit version of spiritual truths about money when we have access to the real deal!

According to the Oxford Dictionary, a "mindset" is the established set of attitudes held by someone.[1] Well, that's sobering, it's an attitude! Jesus gave thirty-nine parables in the Bible and eleven of them were about money. How did He know we would need guidance on personal finances and spending habits? I think it's because money can be an idol or a gift and we get to choose by our attitude which path we take.

The Heart

In the parable of the soil, Jesus talks about four different types of soil and what happens when a farmer goes out to sow seeds. The soil represents your heart and the response it has to the seed or the gospel. Jesus first mentions soil with hard ground where the enemy snatches away the seed of the gospel before it has a chance to take root (Matthew 13:20). Second, He mentions soil with rocky places that is too shallow for faith to survive (Mathew 13:21). Third, He mentions soil with thorns where there are too many idols competing for space leaving no room for seeds of the gospel to grow (Matthew 13:22). His fourth and last example is good soil, ground where the gospel can take root, flourish and reproduce thirty, sixty, and one hundred fold (Matthew 13:23).

I think we all want to be the fourth kind of soil, experiencing a hundredfold blessing and to have a heart that is teachable, willing, and humble. But how do we know if we have good soil or not? We may think our own ways are right, but the Lord is the One who judges the heart of a man (Proverbs 21:2). Just like fire is used to test the purity of silver or gold, the Lord Himself is the one who tests our hearts (Proverbs 17:3). The best way to tend to the soil of your heart is to follow Jesus' instruction on the most important commands given by God. When asked by a teacher of the law which command was the most important, Jesus responded to the teacher and told him:

"Love the Lord your God with all your heart and with all your soul and with all your mind and with all your strength. The second is this: Love your neighbor as yourself. There is no commandment greater than these, of loving the Lord with all our heart, soul, and strength and our neighbor as our self" (Matthew 22:36-40).

Love is the foundation to having good soil and a heart God can trust with His increase. Proverbs 23:12 tells us to apply our hearts to instruction and our ears to words of knowledge. Jesus' response to the teacher of the law is a word of instruction for you to love. Doing this will keep you from being filled with offense. It will also free you from anything trying to snatch the seeds of blessings that are supposed to be rooted in your heart and life.

Jealousy and Judgements

In the parable of the workers in the vineyard, Jesus tells of a landowner who went out and hired workers from morning until late afternoon to tend to his vineyard. When evening came, the landowner instructed his foreman to pay all the workers one denarius regardless of what time they began their work in the day. The men who were the first ones there were grumbling and upset they were paid the same as others who had only worked one hour (Matthew 20:1-12). Jesus concludes the story of the business owner by posing a question in Matthew 20:13 when He asks, "Don't I have the right to do what I want with my own money? Or are you envious because I am generous?"

Comparison leads to jealousy.

One common lie jealous people often succumb to is believing that if someone else has more, then there will never be enough for them. Having this attitude limits your ability to receive what God has for you because it's judgment (Matthew 7:1-2). Think about the thousands of cities around America who have installed dams with the purpose of blocking water. Having judgement and jealousy against others is similar to a large wall-like dam with the water representing your blessings and the dam representing your judgement. Jesus warns us not to judge or we will be judged with the same measure (Luke 6:37). Sowing and reaping goes beyond giving and making money, it is a spiritual principle that applies to our words and attitudes as well. You are not the judge or the jury of someone else's finances. Do not let the seeds of covetousness take root within your soul because it reaps an ugly and bitter harvest you do not want in your life. The inward feeling of jealousy usually stems from fear, and fear is a liar. Fear robs you of the truth about who your Heavenly Father is and who you are as His royal son or daughter.

Proverbs 27:4 says, "Anger is cruel and fury overwhelming, but who can stand before jealousy?" When you are tempted to compare or you feel jealous, refrain from being destructive with your thoughts and words. We are in this world but not of it and jealousy is a worldly characteristic (1 Corinthians 3:3). Instead of comparing and trying to count other people's money, let your heart be inspired when you see others who have more than you, knowing we serve a generous God. Kingdom economics does not always look the same as what our upbringing or culture has taught us. Most of us have been told we get what we deserve. In God's kingdom, you reap where you have not sown, situations that look impossible become possible, and doors of favor open when they appear to be shut.

The Narrow Gate

A common scripture used to fuel the belief that having money is bad and if you are rich you won't get into heaven is when Jesus said, "It is easier for a camel to go through the eye of a needle then a rich man entering the Kingdom of God" (Matthew 19:24). Many believers read that and think, "I better not be rich if I plan on going to heaven." At the time Jesus made this statement people in the Hebrew culture believed if you had wealth you were considered favored and blessed by God. There was a direct connection to God being pleased with you and your level of prosperity. For Jesus to say it was hard for a rich man to enter God's Kingdom was counter cultural because they thought it was an automatic entrance ticket. In addition to that, Jerusalem has a very narrow gate called the eye of a needle and He was probably speaking about the actual gate. The gate is so small the baggage on a camel's back had to be removed and then the camel needed to stoop down in order to fit through. I think Jesus is using imagery to let the Hebrews know being rich doesn't guarantee entrance into heaven like they thought it did. More importantly, this scripture conveys to us that if you do desire to enter His kingdom then you must be willing to lay down your possessions, get low, and have a humble heart. When you humble yourself under God's mighty hand, He will lift you up in His perfect time (1 Peter 5:6).

Through the Lens of Poverty

Poverty is living in bondage and God wants you to live in freedom. When you hear the word poverty you might be thinking of the people who are on welfare and food stamps. Their experience is literal, but what I am referring to is a poverty mindset. It is the belief you will never have enough regardless of how much you have in the bank. The poverty mindset will influence financial decisions and put limits on every area of your life. Fortunately, you don't have to stay imprisoned by this way of thinking.

When the Lord spoke to the Israelites before they entered the promised land, He reminded them that He brought them out of Egypt, referring to it as a place of bondage. He said the Israelites would receive flourishing cities they did not build, houses filled with goods they did not make, wells providing water they did not dig, and vineyards and olive groves they did not plant (Deuteronomy 6:10-12). Just like the Israelites, your resources are not limited when God is your Source. Proverbs 10:22 says, "The blessing of the Lord brings wealth, and He adds no sorrow with it."

In the Bible the Lord is referred to as El Roi which means, "The God who sees me" (Genesis 16:13-14). Meaning, you are seen and known by the Creator of the universe. It is possible to break free from viewing life through the lens of poverty. God sees you and He wants you to live in freedom. Jesus came to set you free and offer encouragement when He said, "What is impossible with man is possible with God" (Luke 18:27)! Survival mode is not your life calling and having a poverty mindset does not equate to being spiritual. The body of Christ needs you. We need you to be in a good financial position so when God asks you to do the impossible, give radically, or take a financial risk, you do it.

Some people feel they received the short end of the stick in life because their parents, grandparents, and great grandparents all had financial hardships. The family you were born into and the upbringing you experienced does not have to limit your ability to change the poverty narrative.

It starts with you. You can be the change.

God Can Bless It

In the book of Genesis, when Jacob negotiated his wages with his father-in-law Laban, Jacob said he would take the brown lambs as well as the speckled and spotted sheep and goats. These animals were considered less valuable since they had blemishes and could not be used for ceremonial sacrifices. Of course Laban agreed to Jacob's offer because Laban would be getting the better end of the deal. But you know what happened next? Jacob became exceedingly prosperous, had large flocks, gained female and male servants, and camels and donkeys! If the speckled were his wages, then all the flocks bore speckled. If the streaked were his wages, then all the flocks bore streaked (Genesis 31:8). In short, whatever is in front of you, God can bless it even if it is not the standard of what people think you need in order to be financially successful. Do not let the opinions of this culture or how you were raised restrict what you do in life.

As a man thinks in his heart, so he is (Proverbs 23:7) so if your beliefs about money don't line up with God's word then it's time to make a change and start dreaming with Jesus! Ask Him what He desires for your life and your finances. Come to God with open hands and a willing heart for the purposes He has destined for you to accomplish. Changing a belief system to line up with the word of God requires daily meditation on scripture. Romans 12:2 instructs us to, "Be transformed by the renewing of your mind and then you will be able to test and approve what God's will is for you. His good, pleasing and perfect will for your life." To help you get started, I included a list of scriptures about finances on the last page of this book for you to meditate on, memorize, and declare over your life. Doing this will help you begin to discover the spiritual truth's about money.

Who Will You Serve?

Raise your hand if you want to be trusted with wealth! I'm talking about the kind of financial prosperity that can be passed down to your children and their children's children. Friends, to be trusted with that big of a gift our hearts can only

have one master. Remember the story when the Lord gave
Moses the ten commandments? Three months after God parted
the Red Sea the Israelites found themselves at the base of
Mount Sinai (Exodus 19:1-2). The miracle of bringing them out
of Egypt is celebrated to this day by Jewish people around the
world through the yearly festival of Passover. After they
experienced a mighty work of God firsthand and are safely en
route to the promised land, the Lord decides to speak audibly to
every single Israelite. God Himself declares the ten
commandments to all the people at Mount Sinai (Exodus 20: 1-
17). Can you imagine? There was thunder, lightning, and even
the sound of trumpets when He was speaking (Exodus 20:18).
The Lord could have, at any point, spoken to the people but He
chose this moment in history to do it.

The very first instruction He gave was, "You shall have
no other gods before me" (Exodus 20:3). After audibly
communicating all ten commandments to the people, the Lord
meets with Moses and reiterates it again. The Lord said to
Moses, "Tell the Israelites this: You have seen for yourselves
that I have spoken to you from heaven: Do not make any gods
to be alongside me; **do not make for yourselves gods of
silver or gods of gold**" (Exodus 20:22-23 emphasis added).
Perhaps, what the Lord spoke to the Israelites that day on
Mount Sinai is why about eight hundred years later Shadrach,
Meshach, and Abednego had the conviction not to bow down to
a ninety-foot golden statue King Nebuchadnezzar set up (Daniel
3:1-12).

Silver and gold are a commodity today just as they were
in the time of Moses. These metals have always represented
something of value that can be used to purchase or barter goods

and services. It sounds silly to me that someone would put their trust in a lifeless carved piece of wood or a gold statue, but it's not much different from putting our trust in money which has no life in it either. Jesus poses a question in Luke 16:10-12 MSG when He said, "If you're honest in small things, you will be honest in big things; If you're a crook in small things, you will be a crook in big things. If you are not honest in small jobs, who will put you in charge of the store?" Jesus responds to this question in the very next verse when He said you cannot serve both God and money (Luke 16:13).

Who you serve will determine how much you are trusted with.

Sometimes I consider what Jesus didn't say versus what He did say. Why did He use the comparison of God and money when He could have said you cannot serve God and women, God and approval of man, or God and political power? Jesus knew if people worshiped money the idol of greed and pride would take root in their hearts. He warns us to be on guard against all kinds of greed because life is not just about having an abundance of possessions (Luke 12:15). If anything, like money, gets between you and God, do something about it. You will be held accountable before the Lord for how you handled your finances on earth, regardless of the amount. Pride says, more possessions, more money, and more "silver and gold" will define your importance. Humility says, God is more significant than any worldly resource and your importance is in your identity as His son or daughter.

A Multitude of Blessings

We serve a God who wants to bless us and when He speaks, His word does not return void (Isaiah 55:11). We learn of an incredible blessing given from God about a month before Moses died. The Lord commanded Moses to declare a covenant blessing to the children of Israel before they entered the promised land with Joshua as their leader. What Moses proclaimed to the Israelites was an overflow of promises. Moses told them the following would come upon them and overtake them:

"Blessed shall you be in the city, and blessed shall you be in the country.

Blessed shall be the fruit of your body, the produce of your ground and the increase of your herds, the increase of your cattle and the offspring of your flocks.

Blessed shall be your basket and your kneading bowl.

Blessed shall you be when you come in, and blessed shall you be when you go out.

The Lord will cause your enemies who rise against you to be defeated before your face; they shall come out against you one way and flee before you seven ways.

The Lord will command the blessing on you in your storehouses and in all to which you set your hand, and He will bless you in the land which the Lord your God is giving you.

The Lord will establish you as a holy people to Himself, just as He has sworn to you, if you keep the commandments of the Lord your God and walk in His ways. Then all peoples of the earth shall see that you are called by the name of the Lord, and they shall be afraid of you.

And the Lord will grant you plenty of goods, in the fruit of your body, in the increase of your livestock, and in the produce of your ground, in the land of which the Lord swore to your fathers to give you.

The Lord will open to you His good treasure, the heavens, to give the rain to your land in its season, and to bless all the work of your hand. You shall lend to many nations, but you shall not borrow.

And the Lord will make you the head and not the tail; you shall be above only, and not be beneath, if you heed the commandments of the Lord your God, which I command you today, and are careful to observe them" (Deuteronomy 28:2-13 emphasis added).

Moses spoke a blessing on their influence, children, reproductive health, businesses, daily life, physical protection, finances, and literally everything they put their hand to. His last statement, "He sends the rain and He blesses the works of their hands" (Genesis 28:12) is an important reminder that God is the Source of it all. The good news is, you do not have to be Jewish to share in these blessings. More good news, not one word has failed of all His good promises, which He spoke through Moses His servant (1 Kings 8:56).

Faith and Identity

By faith you have access to every blessing and promise in the Bible because you are an heir. No matter how wild your past is, you are still grafted into the family and you get to share in all the promises of Christ. Ephesians 3:6 says, "This mystery is that through the gospel the **Gentiles are heirs together with Israel**, members together of one body, and sharers together in the promise in Christ Jesus." The Apostle Paul wrote about half of the New Testament, his accomplishments looked great on paper and yet, he tells us we should not find our confidence or identity in our achievements. When he wrote to the Philippians, he told them, "If someone else thinks they have reasons to put confidence in the flesh, I have more: circumcised on the eighth day, of the people of Israel, of the tribe of Benjamin, a Hebrew of Hebrews; in regard to the law, a Pharisee; as for zeal, I persecuted the church; as for righteousness based on the law, I am faultless" (Philippians 3:4-6). As you can see, the Apostle Paul checked off every box to feel righteous and important in the society he was living in. From the outside looking in, most would think that he deserved to be blessed by God because he had earned it. But you know what he said about his own accolades? He considered it all garbage and said righteousness doesn't come from the law but from faith in Christ (Philippians 3:8-9).

Imagine your dad is the King of England. You would be a royal heir and have access to all the blessings and benefits that a prince or princess enjoys. It works the same way with Jesus but our Heavenly Father is the King of Eternity (1 Timothy 1:17) and you are a citizen of heaven (Ephesians 2:19). If you have put your faith in Jesus Christ as your Lord and Savior, you are a chosen people, a royal priesthood, a holy nation, and God's special possession, that you may declare the praises of him who called you out of darkness into his wonderful light (1 Peter 2:9). The Creator who spoke the world into existence, the One who owns it all is your Provider, your Protector, and your Redeemer.

~~~

The spiritual key which unlocks a true biblical mindset about money is having a heart postured in *Humility*, knowing who you are and Who your source is. Proverbs 22:4 TPT says, "Laying your life down in tender surrender before the Lord will bring life, prosperity, and honor as your reward."

Actions Steps

Write down what you believe to be true about money. Are there any mindsets that surprised you? Are there any areas you would like to work on? Take some time to pray and ask the Lord for guidance. If you already know what you need to do then make a plan and share it with your spouse or a trusted friend for accountability.

How do you know if Jesus is the Lord of your life, qualifying you for the covenant blessings?

The Apostle Paul tells us, "If you **confess with your mouth the Lord Jesus and believe in your heart** that God has raised Him from the dead, you will be saved. For with the heart one believes unto righteousness, and with the mouth confession is made unto salvation. For the Scripture says, 'Whoever believes in Him will not be put to shame.' **For there is no distinction between Jew and Greek**, for the same Lord over all is rich to all who call upon Him. For whoever calls on the name of the Lord shall be saved" (Romans 10:9-13 emphasis added). Take a moment to say this prayer and accept Jesus as your Lord and Savior and by faith, you will be saved!

Salvation Prayer:

Jesus, I believe you are the Son of God, that you died on the cross to rescue me from sin and death and rose from the dead to restore me to God the Father. I choose to turn from my sins and I choose to dedicate my life to you. I receive Your forgiveness and ask You to be my Savior and Lord. Fill me with Your love and restore me. Live in me. Love through me. In Jesus' name I pray. Amen!

How do you change a belief system that does not line up with God's word?

Transforming a belief system is hard. You have to be self aware enough to realize the problem and then choose to make a change. The first step is to renew your mind by reading, meditating, and praying on scripture. To help get you started, I offer a list of scriptures at the end of the book. I encourage you to read them out loud because when you speak His words, they become a sword (Ephesians 6:17).

Were you taught being poor made you more spiritual and having wealth meant you can't be close to God?

There are many people in the Bible who were wealthy and used mightily by God (refer to Chapter 2 on generational wealth). Your level of spirituality or closeness with God is not dependent on being poor or rich. Having a spiritual relationship with Jesus is about spending time with Him so you can be more like Him; it's not about your bank account.

James said to come near to God and He will come near to you (James 4:8). Choosing humility and aligning your beliefs with scripture by spending time reading the Bible will help you get close to Jesus. 1 John 2:4-6 said the test in personally knowing Jesus is this: "Now by this we know that we know Him, if we keep His commandments. He who says, 'I know Him,' and does not keep His commandments, is a liar, and the truth is not in him. But whoever keeps His word, truly the love of God is perfected in him. By this we know that we are in Him. He who says he abides in Him ought himself also to walk just as Jesus walked."

Chapter Two

Generational Wealth

I was raised in a traditional Jewish home. I went to a Jewish Sunday school for most of my life, celebrated all the Jewish holidays, was Bat-Mitzvahed, I learned to read and write Hebrew, and frequented Israel. The major difference between the Sunday school experience most Christians had and mine was the fact that I was only taught from the Old Testament.

Fortunately, my Mother who is also Jewish, accepted Jesus as her savior before I was born and became a Messianic Jew. She is the person who taught me about Yeshua, Jesus' name in Hebrew, in our home when I was growing up. Knowing about her decision to follow Jesus, my Jewish Father made a deal with my mom. My dad told her, "You can have your faith in Jesus, but our children are being raised with Jewish customs and holidays!" She agreed and almost fifty years later, my parents are still married and continue to honor the biblical festivals as Messianic Jews. I share this with you so you know, I am writing this book from a Jewish upbringing and a heart that loves Jesus.

Generational Wealth is Your Inheritance

Generational wealth is anything of value that is passed down from one generation to the next. The first transfer of generational wealth we see in the Bible is within the family line of Abraham, Isaac, and Jacob (Genesis 25:5 ; 27:37). It is the framework God chose to establish and I believe He gave us this example of how generational wealth is transferred so we could learn from it and follow it. Did you know that all children of God have access to the same promises given to Abraham, Isaac, and Jacob? That includes the calling and ability to build, give, and inherit wealth. God does not require you to be biologically related to Abraham, Isaac, or Jacob to experience the financial promises and blessings given to these patriarch's and their descendants. The Apostle Paul writes in Galatians 3:14, "God redeemed you in order that the **blessing given to Abraham might come to the Gentiles through Jesus**, so that by faith you can receive the promise of the Spirit" (emphasis added). Paul told us that it is through faith by grace we are guaranteed the promises, not just to those who are of the law (Hebrew or Jewish) but also to those who have faith like Abraham because Abraham is the father of us all (Romans 4:16).

Did you catch that? It is by faith you can receive the blessings that were given to Abraham and it is through Jesus you have access to them. You don't have to earn it, work for it, or strive to attain it. Abraham, Isaac, and Jacob were beneficiaries blessed by God and vessels the Lord used to pass the blessing on to others. As a child of God through faith, you are also an heir and the beneficiary of the same blessings that God provided for these men and their families.

The purpose of financial favor is to bless others with it.

It must be given away for it to be used effectively. This can be accomplished by establishing generational wealth for your family. This chapter will give biblical history and insight to help you understand how anyone, not just those born of a Jewish bloodline, can walk in the promise of the inheritance of generational wealth. Practical steps to do this can be found in Chapter 4 on saving and investing, but in this chapter, we will embark on the spiritual application of it.

Wealth of Abraham and Lot

It started with Abram, whose name would eventually be changed to Abraham. The Lord spoke to Abram and told him:

"Go from your country, your people and your father's household to the land I will show you. I will make you into a great nation, and I will bless you; I will make your name great, and you will be a blessing. I will bless those who bless you, and whoever curses you I will curse; **and all peoples on earth will be blessed through you**" (Genesis 12:1-3 emphasis added).

The Bible says Abram, at 75 years old, obeyed and left Babylon (modern day Iraq). Then he went on the journey towards Canaan (modern day Israel) with his wife, servants, possessions, and his nephew Lot. Lot's father Haran, was Abram's deceased brother so Abram took responsibility for his nephew Lot whose life was richly blessed simply by being associated with Abram. As promised, God told Abram He would bless those who bless Abram and He certainly did! The wealth of Abram and Lot was eventually so great, they had to separate because the land could not contain all the animals, tents, and herdsmen they both owned (Genesis 13:5-6). Since the land was not large enough for both men, Lot left Abram and went his own way.

A New Name and Promises Given

God's blessing was on Abram and he became very wealthy in livestock, silver, and in gold (Genesis 13:2). The Lord made a powerful covenant with Abram by changing his name and giving him many notable promises (Genesis 15: 1-17). There are only four times in the entire Bible when God decided to change someone's name. When He did, it was intentional and done with a divine purpose for their new identity. This was one of those times. The Lord changed Abram's name to Abraham which means, "Father of a multitude" and changed his wife Sarai's name to Sarah which means, "princess." God told Abraham that He would be his shield, bring increase to his life, make him fruitful, nations and kings would come from his seed, and assured him that his reward would be very great. God also promised his descendants would be as numerous as the stars in the sky and even though Abraham had no biological children at the time, Abraham believed God and his faith was counted unto him as righteousness (Genesis 15:1-6). The Lord asked

Abraham to do one thing in return — circumcise every male in his household. This was a sign of the covenant between God, Abraham, and his descendants. It was considered a covenant of flesh.

I think the oath God made to bless, protect, and increase Abraham's life was amazing. It seemed unfathomable since he had no biological children, but the Lord boldly told Abraham a son named Isaac would be born from his wife Sarah. At the time, Abraham was 99 years of age and wasn't sure of the possibility of his 90 year old wife bearing a child. Fortunately, the destiny and purpose of Isaac's life was grounded in God's promise and it came to pass just as He had spoken (Genesis 17:2-7).

Isaiah 43:7 tells us, "Everyone who is called by My name, whom I have created for My glory; I have formed him, yes, I have made him." Just like Isaac, you were formed for God's glory. Your destiny and purpose are grounded in that truth. The Bible doesn't say why God originally chose to make an everlasting oath with Abraham and his descendants. It only mentions Abraham's faith against all odds and a heart that believed what the Lord had spoken when circumstances said otherwise. The basis of the generational wealth God intended to bestow on Abraham's family started with faith and trust in the Lord's character. Abraham was in agreement with the heart of God for his life in spite of what his earthly situation looked like.

God Wants to Provide For You

There are many names used for God in the Bible and these names are meant to reveal parts of God's nature. We first learn of the name Jehovah Jireh, from Abraham which means, "The Lord is my Provider." Several years after Sarah bore Isaac, God asked Abraham to do the unthinkable; sacrifice his son! So, Abraham took his son Isaac and two servants and traveled up to Mount Moriah but didn't say a word about what God instructed him to do to Isaac. We don't know the internal dialogue Abraham was having after he had built the altar and tied his son to it. We do know, at the exact moment he was going to put the knife to his son's throat, an angel of the Lord stopped him from killing Isaac and a ram was provided in his son's place (Genesis 22:9-14). It was at this moment Abraham declared; the Lord is my Provider!

There is a reason Abraham is called the Father of Faith.

Hebrews 11:17-19 tells us, "By faith Abraham, when God tested him, offered Isaac as a sacrifice. He who had embraced the promises was about to sacrifice his one and only son, even though God had said to him, 'It is through Isaac that your offspring will be reckoned.' **Abraham reasoned that God could even raise the dead**, and so in a manner of speaking he did receive Isaac back from death" (emphasis added).

Abraham's profound faith introduced us to God as our Provider and Abraham's faith solidified generational blessings that would be passed down through his descendants. His one action of surrender had a ripple effect we are still experiencing to this day. We serve a God who Provides. It's His name, it's His character, and it's His desire to provide for you.

Wealth of Isaac and Ishmael

Before Abraham and Sarah had Isaac, Sarah was weary of waiting on God's promise for a child. Twenty five years had passed since God promised her and Abraham a son and she was still infertile. Sarah made a suggestion to Abraham and told him, "The Lord has kept me from having children. Go, sleep with my maidservant Hagar; perhaps I can build a family through her" (Genesis 16:2). Abraham listened to her, slept with Hagar, and she conceived a son named Ishmael. This is why Isaac and Ishmael have different Mothers but they share the same father, Abraham. Both sons experienced financial blessings but the full inheritance and all that Abraham owned was left only to Isaac (Genesis 25:5). Isaac, God's promised son to Abraham and Sarah, inherited an abundance of wealth including sheep, cattle, silver, gold, servants, camels, and donkeys (Genesis 34:35-36).

Every aspect of Isaac's life was blessed. When Isaac planted crops in the land, he reaped a hundredfold the same year **because the Lord's blessing was on his life** (Genesis 26:12 emphasis added). A hundredfold is not a normal increase for crops! Can you imagine having that type of miracle working increase in your life? Everything Isaac put his hand to prospered and he became extremely rich with his wealth growing year after year (Genesis 26:13). This example of generational wealth is evidence of God not only wanting your resources to be financially blessed, but for it to multiply after it's given to your children.

You Can Multiply the Inheritance

There were seven wells Isaac's father Abraham dug during his lifetime. Genesis 26:18 tells us that Isaac decided to reopen the wells that were dug by his father, which the Philistines who were enemies of Israel had filled with dirt. Wells served as a resource of water for animals and people, but they were also a place to socialize, do business transactions, and even where Isaac would find his wife Rebekah. There was only one problem, after Isaac opened the wells back up the local Philistines quarreled with him and claimed the wells as their own. Instead of going to war over it, Isaac dug new wells in a different area. He knew he was not limited to only live off of what his father Abraham had accomplished in the previous generation. Isaac understood God's blessing was on him personally. He knew he could flourish in the land and build something that was life-sustaining for his own family, servants, and animals. Isaac took what he had inherited from his father Abraham and multiplied it.

Ishmael, a Recipient of the Blessings

Isaac's half-brother Ishmael had a life of affluence too. His Egyptian mother Hagar fled into the desert and raised him there when he was a teenager. God said He would bless Ishmael, make him fruitful, increase him, make him the father of twelve princes, and into a great nation (Genesis 17:20). Ishmael became a skilled hunter, expert archer, married, and had twelve sons. As promised, the Lord made

Ishmael prosper. Throughout history, descendants of the
Ishmaelites have been known to live in northern Arabia, which
is rich in oil and flowing with wealth to this day.

Wealth of Jacob

Isaac and his wife Rebekah would give birth to twin sons,
Jacob and Esau. Before their birth, Rebekah received a word
from the Lord that the older brother would serve the younger
brother. Since Jacob was born second, he was considered the
youngest and therefore the generational blessing and covenant
would be established through him (Genesis 25:23). Both sons
would experience God's protection and be financially blessed,
but the promise of the coming Messiah would only come
through the seed of Jacob (Numbers 24:17 ; Galatians 3:16).

In a series of events, Jacob manipulated his older
brother Esau into selling him his birthright and deceived his
dying Father Isaac into giving him the blessing instead of giving
it to the eldest, Esau (Genesis 27:33). Obviously, this is not the
best way to fulfill a word received from the Lord. The acts of
deception that were sown would be reaped later on in Jacob's
life. First by his father-in-law Laban who tricked him into
marrying the wrong daughter and later by his ten sons who
deceived him into believing his favorite son Joseph had died.
There was a lot of emotional stress and disappointment in
Jacob's life but nonetheless, the hand of God was on him.

You Serve a God of Unlimited Power

Shortly after receiving the blessing from his father Isaac, Jacob had a prophetic dream from the Lord. In the dream, God said his descendants would be like the dust of the earth spreading out to the north, south, east, and west. The Lord also reiterated the same promise He gave to his grandfather Abraham and told Jacob all people on the earth would be blessed through him and his offspring. Jacob was so amazed and marked by this experience, he changed the name of the city to Bethel which means, "House of God" and committed to give a tenth of everything he made to the Lord (Genesis 28:13-22).

In Jacob's encounter at Bethel, we learn of another name of God. The Lord addresses Himself as El Shaddai, which means, "The Lord Almighty" or having unlimited power and influence. The words that went forth from the Lord's mouth did not return void in Jacob's life or in the life of his descendants. Jacob prospered and those who were related to him prospered as well. He was used as an instrument of God to pass the blessings on to his family. Jacob would go on to marry two sisters, Leah and Rachel and have twelve sons who would become the twelve tribes of Israel.

God's protection and provision over the Jewish people through the centuries has proven He is, in fact, the God of unlimited power and influence. Even when the Jewish people rebelled and served other gods, the Lord was gracious to them. Even when rulers and kings tried to annihilate and wipe out the Jewish people from the earth, the Lord had compassion and showed concern for them because of His covenant with

Abraham, Isaac, and Jacob. To this day God has been unwilling to destroy or banish them from his presence (2 Kings 13:23).

Israel is Established

Before Jacob died, God appeared to him for the last time at Bethel where He had first talked with him almost one hundred years earlier. The Lord gave Jacob a new name, identity, and a promotion that day. God changed his name from Jacob to Israel and declared Israel would become a great nation, kings would come from his descendants, and vowed to give him the land He promised to Abraham and Isaac (Genesis 35:9-13). Five hundred years later, Joshua fulfilled God's promise and took control of all the land in Canaan. Moses was then instructed by God to give the land Joshua had conquered as an inheritance to Israel, according to their twelve tribal divisions which were the descendants of Jacob (Joshua 11:23).

You Have Access to the Promises

There are many more in scripture who were financially blessed in an abundant way by God. Joseph, David, Solomon, Job, Ruth, and Esther are just a few. In our modern day currency, they would all be millionaires and billionaires. Almost all of their stories include family dysfunction, sexual immorality, murder, jealousy, anger, fear and deception, but His promises are not dependent on our accomplishments. God prospered a lot of imperfect people because He swore an oath and made a covenant. When the Lord spoke, His Word went out to perform His will and it never came up short. God doesn't change His mind (Malachi 3:6) and this fact is echoed in the book of Hebrews when it states Jesus is the same yesterday, today, and forever (Hebrews 13:8). His covenant is from generation to generation and it is everlasting (Genesis 17:7).

In addition to Abraham, Isaac, and Jacob being our first example of generational wealth it should be noted that at the burning bush, Moses asked God who he should tell the Israelites sent him. God instructed Moses to tell them, "The Lord, the God of your fathers; the God of Abraham, the God of Isaac, and the God of Jacob has sent me to you. **This is my name forever**, the name you shall call me from generation to generation" (Exodus 3:15 emphasis added). Then, when Moses was afraid to ask Pharaoh to let the Israelites leave Egypt, God reminded Moses He had appeared to Abraham, Isaac, and Jacob as El Shaddai or God Almighty and established His covenant with them forever (Exodus 6:2-4).

On top of that, Jesus fearlessly declared to the Sadducees that God was, "the God of Abraham, the God of Isaac, and the God of Jacob" (Matthew 22:32). There is significance in the legacy of Abraham, Isaac, and Jacob if God Himself and His son Jesus both acknowledged these men. The covenant Jesus made with us, which was the pouring out of His own blood, is based on His love for us (Matthew 26:26-28). Jesus loves you for a singular reason — He chooses to love you. It is through Jesus all blessings flow because the covenant we have with Jesus, known as the new covenant, is the promise of eternal life (Hebrews 9:15). There is nothing in your past, present, or future that would make Him love you any less. Your worth is in the blood of Jesus which is valuable beyond estimation. God is faithful to

His covenant promises which started with the blood sacrifice the Lord performed for Abraham (Genesis 15:17-21) and carried through to the death and resurrection of Jesus. Not only does God refer to Himself as "The God of Abraham" (Genesis 26:24) but we as believers are "sons in the family of Abraham" (Acts 13:26). The Apostle Paul gives further explanation when he told the Galatians:

"Just as Abraham believed God, and it was accounted to him for righteousness, therefore know that only **those who are of faith are the sons of Abraham**. And the Scripture, foreseeing that God would justify the Gentiles by faith, preached the gospel to Abraham beforehand, saying, 'In you all the nations shall be blessed.' So then those who are of faith are blessed with believing Abraham" (Galatians 3:6-9 emphasis added).

The purpose of our lives is to be a witness to the nations and a blessing to people of all different backgrounds and skin colors. The covenant blessings that started with Abraham and carried on through Jesus are still available to you. The promises God made are inherited by faith and are guaranteed to all of Abraham's offspring! Since you are God's child, He has made you an heir (Galatians 4:7) in the same way Isaac and Jacob were heirs of Abraham. Deuteronomy 8:18 says, "But remember the Lord your God, for it is He who gives you the ability to produce wealth, and so **confirms His covenant**, which He swore to your ancestors, as it is today."

Thankfully, we don't have the legalistic burden of trying to earn what God has promised us. If you have faith in Jesus, you are a true child of Abraham. You are His heir, and God's promises to Abraham also belong to you (Galatians 3:29)! Your inheritance is Jesus and He is the giver of all increase and blessings. The Apostle Paul wrote about your inheritance in his letter to the Ephesians. He told them, **"In Him also we have obtained an inheritance**, being predestined according to the purpose of Him who works all things according to the counsel of His will, that we who first trusted in Christ should be to the praise of His glory"** (Ephesians 1:11-12 emphasis added).

~~~

The spiritual key which opens the door for you and your family to walk in God's covenant promises is *Faith*. Believe His word and pray it over your life, your children, and your finances.

Actions Steps

How to receive the covenant blessings promised through Abraham, Isaac, and Jacob for you and your family:

Isaiah 47:13 says that God's hand laid the foundation of the earth and His right hand stretched out the heavens. He is the Lord Almighty, infinite in power, and wants to bless you. Pray and believe because your faith will be counted as righteousness, just like it was for Abraham because God's promises to Abraham also belong to you (Galatians 3:29).

Is the Old Testament done away with? Do the covenants God

made matter anymore?

Yes, it still matters! The Old Testament had laws and covenant promises. These laws were fulfilled by Jesus which is why, for example, we are not responsible to sacrifice animals anymore. The Apostle Paul tells us, "Christ has redeemed us from the curse of the law, having become a curse for us, for it is written, 'Cursed is everyone who hangs on a tree,' that the blessing of Abraham might come upon the Gentiles in Christ Jesus, that we might receive the promise of the Spirit through faith" (Galatians 3:13-14).

The covenant promises are different from the laws. They are everlasting and perpetual. **God remembers His covenant promises forever** starting with the covenant he made with Abraham and the oath he swore to Isaac (Psalm 105:8-9 emphasis added). See the following illustration for Abraham's Family tree.

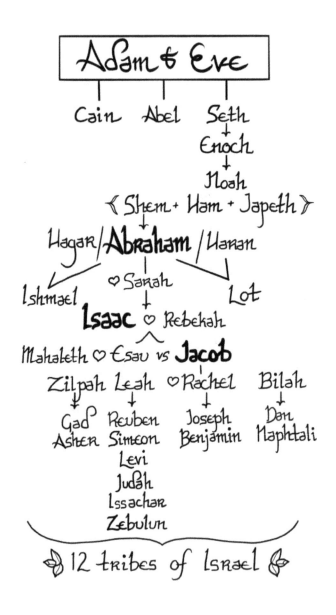

Adam & Eve

Cain   Abel   Seth
                ↓
              Enoch
                ↓
              Noah
        { Shem + Ham + Japeth }
                ↓
Hagar / **Abraham** / Haran
          ♡ Sarah
Ishmael   ↓   Lot
      Isaac ♡ Rebekah

Mahaleth ♡ Esau vs **Jacob**
                        |
Zilpah Leah ♡ Rachel   Bilah
   ↓   ↓   ↓   ↓
 Gad   Reuben   Joseph   Dan
Asher Simeon Benjamin Naphtali
        Levi
        Judah
       Issachar
       Zebulun

❧ 12 tribes of Israel ☙

44

Chapter Three

Giving

*I*n my early twenties I attended a New Year's Eve conference with a group of friends called "One Thing" hosted by the International House of Prayer in Kansas City. The lead Pastor gave a sermon on giving and at the end, he asked if anyone in the room had the desire to be a radical giver, to stand up. You know the feeling when someone nudges you from behind? I experienced something similar as my heart leapt within me because my answer was a resounding "Yes." I stood up to receive the prayer and I'm so thankful I did. It's amazing how one yes changes the course of your walk with God. Even though I grew up with parents who demonstrated giving, something changed in my heart at that conference. I thought my giving muscle was relatively strong until I realized I wasn't dreaming big enough. That night, something shifted. Desires began to rise up in me and I started to dream about buying people cars, buying people houses, and giving extravagantly to ministries who are spreading the gospel. It was as if the Lord marked me with a new purpose in life.

It's funny how God works; the minute you say yes to becoming a radical giver, He is quick to show you there is no shortage of people who need to be blessed financially. You know how bugs are drawn to light? After that night, it was as if people were drawn to me who had certain needs in their life. Suddenly, almost every conversation started with, "I don't know why I'm telling you this but this or that happened and it has financially hurt us." In the beginning, my giving ranged from buying someone's groceries, paying a student's tuition, or even covering the monthly mortgage for a family in need. I realized to be a better steward of the money, I needed to start a nonprofit. So, in 2008 I founded Moving Mountains Charity, a 501-(c)(3) organization. 100% of the proceeds received are given away and I receive no financial compensation as the Director. Through this nonprofit, some of the early dreams I had of giving have come to pass and others are in reach. Let me be clear, sharing this personal information with you is not to impress you. The moment a donation is received by Moving Mountains, it belongs to God. I am simply an ambassador of Jesus who said yes to helping His children when He leads me to.

While I attended the University of Florida's business school, I noticed there was a law school on campus called the Fredric G. Levin College of Law. I can only imagine how many millions of dollars were donated from Mr. Levin to have his name attached to one of the top 25 law schools in the United States. My point is, if the people of the world who don't know Jesus as their savior are willing to give lavishly, then how much more should we, as believers, be willing to give?

Before the Law

The literal meaning of tithe is "one-tenth" or 10%. The
first mention of giving a tithe in the Bible is when Abraham met
Melchizedek, the priest of God Most High. Abraham received
terrible news that his nephew Lot was taken prisoner by four
opposing kings. After Abraham sent men to successfully rescue
Lot and his family, Melchizedek king of Salem showed up with
bread, wine, and words of encouragement. He said, "Blessed be
Abram by God Most High, Creator of heaven and earth and
praise be to God Most High, who delivered your enemies into
your hand. **Then Abram gave him a tenth of everything**"
(Genesis 14:18-20 emphasis added).

The important observation from this encounter is that
Melchizedek is a Christ-like figure. Like Jesus, he was both a
king and a priest. Like Jesus, his name was "king of
righteousness" and "king of peace." And like Jesus, he remains
a priest forever (Hebrews 7:1-3). Abraham knew his victory was
because of the Lord and gave a tenth of the plunder as an act of
gratefulness. Before the Hebrews were instructed to tithe under
the law, Abraham gave from a heart that recognized where his
blessings came from. He acknowledged God was his source and
showed honor by offering a tithe to Melchizedek, who was a
representation of Jesus.

The Law and Tithing

When Moses was leading the Israelites through the
desert, God gave Moses laws to create a set of values and to

separate the Israelites from foreigners who worshiped idols. The first command given from the Lord to tithe is found in Leviticus 27:30. He instructed Moses to tell the people, "A tithe of everything from the land, whether grain from the soil or fruit from the trees, belongs to the Lord: it is holy to the Lord." In the Old Testament under the Mosaic Law, there were three different tithes, each with a different purpose.

The first was a tithe to the Levites. This was because the tribe of Levi was not given any land as an inheritance, though the other eleven tribes were. The Levites were called to work at the tabernacle as priests and bear the responsibility of sins for the nation of Israel. The tithes helped support the temple and the priesthood (Numbers 18: 21-24). The Levites in turn were instructed to give one-tenth of the tithe they received, to the Aaronic Priests who were the sons of Aaron, the brother of Moses (Numbers 18:25-28).

The second tithe was for the feasts, also known in our modern day as Jewish holidays (Deuteronomy 14:22-27). The Levitical law required Israelites to celebrate the feasts honoring the Lord at appointed times throughout the year (Leviticus 23:1-2). There were seven feasts observed annually. They were a shadow of things to come and represent the first and second coming of the Messiah (Colossians 2:16-17). They were celebrated in this order:

1. Passover — Fulfillment: Jesus is our passover lamb and died on this day (1 Corinthians 5:7-8).
2. Unleavened Bread — Fulfillment: Jesus was sinless and was buried on this day (2 Corinthians 5:21).

3. First Fruits —Fulfillment: Jesus resurrected from the dead on this day (1 Corinthians 15:20-23).

4. Pentecost — Fulfillment: The Holy Spirit was poured out on this day (Acts 2:1-4).

5. Trumpets — Not fulfilled: Last trumpet sounds and we meet the Lord in the air (1 Thessalonians 4:16-18).

6. Atonement — Fulfillment: God presented Jesus as a sacrifice of atonement (Romans 3:21-25).

7. Tabernacles — Not fulfilled: Christ literally dwells with man for a thousand years (Revelations 20:6).

The appointed feasts were given about 1,445 years before Christ was born. The Jewish people were prophetically rehearsing what was to come and they didn't even realize it. These festivals were a time of social gatherings, animal sacrifices, and any type of work was prohibited. Some of the celebrations lasted seven days long so although this was an ordinance, it also had a definite expense associated with it. So, how did each household provide for the expense? By setting aside a second tithe! We see in the book of John that even Jesus honored this law. In John 7:10, Jesus celebrated the Feast of Tabernacles. In John 10:22-24, He attended the Feast of Dedication or Hanukkah. And, in John 2:23, He went to the Passover festival in Jerusalem during spring time. Taking into consideration the "Church" began as a Jewish institution and was founded in Judea by the Jews who were followers of Jesus, it is no surprise Jesus and all his disciples took part in the festivals.

The third tithe was for the poor, fatherless, and the widow. This tithe was to be given every third year and stored in the town, similar to a community pantry (Deuteronomy 14:28-29). God wanted those who were less fortunate to be provided and cared for. It's interesting to note, this is the only tithe where God said, if you do it, He will bless the works of your hands (verse 29).

The tithing method in the Old Testament was first to God, second to benefit your own spiritual condition, and finally to your neighbor in need. This gives us a glimpse into God's intent for us to incorporate giving as a way of life.

New Testament Giving

The New Testament is not as direct with the amount or places we are expected to give. Just as Christians are not required to sacrifice animals or observe the ceremonial laws, neither are we required to give an exact percentage of our income. The Apostle Paul offers some direction in 2 Corinthians 9:6-7 when he writes, "Remember this: Whoever sows sparingly will also reap sparingly, and whoever sows generously will also reap generously. Each man should give what he has decided in his heart to give, not reluctantly or under compulsion, for God loves a cheerful giver." In that passage, Paul reminds us of the spiritual principle of sowing and reaping but does not pressure us into a certain amount, instead, he tells us that our giving is something we should decide in our own hearts. We are also encouraged in 1 Corinthians 16:2 to be consistent in our giving because it says, "On the first day of every week, each one of you should set aside a sum of money in keeping with his income."

According to the Non Profit Source, in 2019 only 20% of church attendees tithed and of those tithing, they gave on average, 2.5% of their income.[2] This is a shockingly low statistic considering the principle of tithing is probably the most, if not the only subject taught about money in the American church.

Have you ever known someone who went without meals because their single mom decided to tithe the money instead of purchase groceries? Have you ever known someone who never felt like they were allowed to buy themselves anything fun growing up, but was guilted into tithing? Have you ever known someone who felt embarrassed because they came from a family with money when their friends didn't have as much? Oftentimes, the principle of tithing can trigger a range of emotions in people, some positive and some negative depending on their experience. Whatever your background has been, I hope this chapter helps you gain freedom from giving out of fear, giving out of guilt, or giving to earn the approval of God. I invite you today to explore what true biblical giving can look like in your life.

His Ways are Higher

Most of today's teaching on tithing originates from the tithing system God told Moses to direct the Israelites to follow. However, in Matthew 5:17, Jesus said He came to fulfill the law and the prophets not to abolish them. He knew that no man, in his own strength, would ever be able to keep the law and earn their salvation. After Jesus makes the bold statement of fulfilling the law, which includes the law to tithe, He then proceeds to invite us to a higher level of maturity and grace.

The glaring question is, what percentage of your income should you set aside for giving tithes? Jesus did not flat out tell you but He did give you a new standard to live by which is vastly different from the instruction found in the Old Testament.

For example, Jesus tells us in the Old Testament that murder is when you kill someone, but in the New Testament, murder is when you have anger in your heart towards them (Matthew 5:21-22). He goes on to tell us that in the Old Testament adultery is when a physical act is committed, but in the New Testament it's when you lust after a woman with your eyes (Matthew 5:27). And, Jesus tells us the Old Testament law says to hate your enemy but now, in the New Testament, you are called to love your enemy and to pray for them (Matthew 5:43-44).

So, my question to you is if the law required a 10% tithe and Jesus came to fulfill it and not abolish it, how much more should we give under the grace He has called us to walk in as New Testament believers? This question isn't to shame you, it is an invitation to sincerely reflect on what type of giver you want to be. There could never be a dollar amount on your salvation, your value to God, or what it cost the Father for Jesus to die on the cross and fully satisfy every law of the Old Testament, making salvation available to you and to me. Remember, Christ came not to destroy the old religious system but to build upon it so think about what you want to build with your giving. The impact your charitable giving will make is part of the legacy you leave behind. It is living out the greatest command; to love your neighbor as yourself.

God Fund

I cannot be the Holy Spirit and tell you what percentage to set aside for giving or if you should give before taxed or after taxed money. God has a definite plan for your finances so pray and seek Him on how to steward it wisely because He will honor your actions. If you are not ready to have a nonprofit, then start by opening a separate savings account and transfer over a percentage of your household income each month. Once you do this, you will officially have a God fund! A God fund is a specific amount of money set aside purposely for giving. This is where life starts to get really fun. There is so much joy that comes from giving!

Give to your local church, give when you hear of needs in your community, give to ministries that protect women and children, and sow into the things that move the heart of God from your God fund. Proverbs 3:9 says, "Honor the Lord with your wealth, with the first fruits of all your crops; then your barns will be filled to overflowing, and your vats will brim over with new wine." Abraham led by example because he honored the Lord with his wealth by giving a tenth of it away before there was a command that required him to. Similarly, you are also not under the law and your God fund is the recognition that you trust the Lord with your finances. When you are willing to partner with Him to influence and shape culture with your giving, the reward is eternal.

Heavenly Treasures

In Matthew 6:19-21, Jesus said to store up your treasures in heaven where moth and vermin do not destroy. This was a strong statement for the Hebrew culture of that day because their focus was accumulating wealth and gaining influence on earth. The things we treasure are directly related to the condition of our heart. In Colossians 3:2 it says, set your minds on things that are above, not on things that are on earth. If we have a transformed heart that values eternal treasures more than worldly possessions, we will bring glory to God instead of ourselves. Jesus is not a vending machine where you insert money expecting a certain item to appear out of the bottom compartment.

Give with the attitude that your God fund is God's money in the form of a treasure box. Your job is to give the treasures away. The Apostle Paul reiterates Jesus' desire about where we should lay up our treasures when he said, "Command those who are rich in this present world not to be arrogant nor to put their hope in wealth, which is so uncertain, but to put their hope in God, who richly provides us with everything for our enjoyment. Command them to do good, to be rich in good deeds, and to be generous and willing to share. In this way they will lay up treasure for themselves as a firm foundation for the coming age, so that they may take hold of the life that is truly life" (1 Timothy 6:17-19). You might sow your time and resources into people and ministries but some of your reward is given when you get to heaven. Other seeds you sow, your reward may be given to you on earth. We will never really know the full extent and impact our giving made until we face our Heavenly Father one day.

If your heart has been wounded by teachings on giving, ask God to heal you and forgive those who have caused you pain. Do not let the actions of others that may have jaded your beliefs result in you opting out of your assignment from God to be a giver. Proverbs 19:17 says, "Whoever is kind to the poor lends to the Lord and he will reward them for what they have done. Your reward is from the Lord, not from people.

Say it out loud with me:
"My reward is from the Lord, not from people."

Give freely with no expectations of getting anything in return. When Jesus was having dinner at a prominent Pharisee's house, He told the parable of the banquet while He was there. He spoke to the host and said it is better to invite the poor, crippled, lame, and blind then your friends when you host a party, and by doing this the **Lord Himself will bless you and repay you** since they cannot (Luke 14:13-14 emphasis added). It's better to get our reward from the One who owns everything and knows everything (Psalm 24:1-2) than from people who will fail you.

Practice Generosity

During harvest time it was customary for the Israelites to leave the edges of their fields untouched when the harvest came in. The reason they did this is because the Lord told them to let the poor and foreigners gather the harvest on the corners of their fields (Leviticus 23:22). Giving some of their crops to people they did not know or have a relationship with was practicing generosity.

> Giving is a muscle that has to be continually strengthened.

In Deuteronomy 15:11 the Lord says, "There will always be poor people in the land. Therefore, I command you to be openhanded toward your fellow Israelites who are poor and needy." James makes the point that you may have faith in Jesus, but how impactful is your faith if you hear of needs you can meet and do nothing about it? In James 2:15-16 he says, "What good is it, my brothers and sisters, if someone claims to have faith but has no deeds? Can such faith save them? Suppose a brother or a sister is without clothes and daily food. If one of you says to them, 'Go in peace; keep warm and well fed,' but does nothing about their physical needs, what good is it?"

At the end of the book of Romans we see the church giving money to the Apostle Paul to bring to the Jewish believers in Jerusalem. Paul said, "For it pleased those from Macedonia and Achaia to make a certain contribution for the poor among the saints who are in Jerusalem. It pleased them indeed, and they are their debtors. For if the Gentiles have been partakers of their spiritual things, **their duty is also to minister to them in material things**" (Romans 15:26-27 emphasis added). The one group of people Paul considered important and is straight forward about giving to is your fellow believer who is in need. Just like the early church who sold their possessions and distributed the money to those who were less fortunate (Acts 2:45), there is always someone you can bless. Buying lunch for the person behind you, leaving a tip that matches the bill for your waitress, and keeping a zip lock bag filled with socks, granola bars, and a water bottle for the next homeless person you see are small actions we can take to practice generosity in our everyday life. Proverbs 11:23 says, "A generous person will prosper, whoever refreshes others will be refreshed."

Practice Compassion

We all know the story of Sodom and Gomorrah. It was a city so full of sin and spiritual blindness that the Lord sent fire from heaven to destroy all the people and the land. Because of Abraham's favor and friendship with God, his nephew Lot and immediate family were spared but no one else came out alive (Genesis 19:24-25). When you think of the sins they were killed for, sexual immorality and idolatry probably come to mind. But the Lord also held it against them that they had no compassion or concern for the poor. It is addressed in the book of Ezekiel about fourteen hundred years after Sodom was destroyed. In this book, the Lord told a prophet and priest named Ezekiel to bring some bad news to the Israelites who were living in Jerusalem. Ezekiel was instructed to rebuke them because they had broken their covenant with God and were sacrificing their children to idols. God even went as far as comparing their sins to Sodom and Gomorrah. In the comparison the Lord said, "Now this was the sin of your sister Sodom: She and her daughters were arrogant, **overfed and unconcerned; they did not help the poor and needy**. They were haughty and did detestable things before me. Therefore, I did away with them as you have seen" (Ezekiel 16:49-50 emphasis added). Notice the Lord was grieved about more than just sexual immorality and idol worship. Do you know anyone who is arrogant and has more than enough but is unconcerned with the poor and needy? Don't be like them! Practice compassion and give when you see the poor in need.

Giving Brings Protection

It's important to know, giving brings walls of protection around your life. A lot of the language in the Bible about giving is compared to farming. Sow seeds today and reap a harvest next season or the following. A common trait that the Lord tells us we will reap when we give is protection. He speaks about protection from trouble in Psalm 41:1 which says, "Oh, the joys of those who are kind to the poor! The Lord rescues them when they are in trouble." He speaks about protection from greed in Proverbs 21:26 which says, "Some people are always greedy for more, but the godly love to give." He speaks about protection over your work in Deuteronomy 15:10 which says, "Give generously to them and do so without a grudging heart; then because of this the Lord your God will bless you in all your work and in everything you put your hand to." He speaks about protection over your finances in Malachi 3:11 which says, "I will prevent pests from devouring your crops, and the vines in your fields will not drop their fruit before it is ripe, says the Lord Almighty."

Let's take a deeper look at Malachi Chapter 3 and the context it was written in. There is a lot more covered in this passage than just having your finances protected.

"I the Lord do not change. So, you, the descendants of Jacob, are not destroyed. Ever since the time of your ancestors you have turned away from my decrees and have not kept them. Return to me, and I will return to you, says the Lord Almighty.

But you ask, 'How are we to return?' Will a mere mortal rob God? Yet you rob me. But you ask, 'How are we robbing you?' In tithes and offerings. You are under a curse, your whole nation, because you are robbing me.

Bring the whole tithe into the storehouse, that there may be food in my house. **Test me in this, says the Lord Almighty, and see if I will not throw open the floodgates of heaven and pour out so much blessing that there will not be room enough to store it.**

I will prevent pests from devouring your crops, and the vines in your fields will not drop their fruit before it is ripe, says the Lord Almighty. Then all the nations will call you blessed, for yours will be a delightful land, says the Lord Almighty" (Malachi 3:6-12 emphasis added).

Malachi is the final chapter in the Old Testament and it's the last message God gives before 400 years of silence. It was written in a time when tithes were supposed to be given to God from the proceeds of land, herds, and flocks. Giving a tenth of their possessions was an act that recognized God as both the source and owner of all their blessings. During this time, the Israelites were not following the Levitical law to tithe or any laws for that matter, so God chose Malachi whose name means "messenger" to do just that, give His people a message. The book is only four chapters long but it is packed with accusations from the Lord towards the Israelites because of the many sins they were committing. Some of the sins include corrupting the covenant, adultery, sorcery, perjury, not tithing, and living in rebellion. He could have made a big deal out of any of the sins being committed but God chose to put his finger on tithing.

It was the litmus test of the condition of their hearts.

As if the situation couldn't get any worse, He addresses the people as descendants of Jacob instead of descendants of Israel. God changed Jacob's name to Israel and by doing so it gave him a new identity and purpose in life. In Hebrew, Jacob means "supplant or undermine" and the name Israel means "triumphant with God." I think this was done deliberately to point out they were not living in the fulfillment of their destiny. Israel was called to be blessed and to be a blessing to the nations (Genesis 12:2). In this moment in history, the denial of God's rightful ownership to their possessions was undermining His plan for them to be living the triumphant life He had purposed for them. He even goes as far to say, "You are under a curse because you are robbing me." Whoa. I would rather give 10% of something than have 100% of it be under a curse.

Finally, God gives a challenge by asking the people to test Him and find out what will happen when they tithe. God was letting the Israelites know He sees everything, He knows everything, and He wants to abundantly bless them, but He can't until they stop being greedy, get their hearts right with Him, and start giving.

Take a moment to think about Mary, Joanna, and Suzanna who were the three women that helped fund Jesus' ministry (Luke 8:2-3). Can you imagine feeding thirteen men and making sure they had a place to sleep for three years? That is no small feat and takes real finances. This is how God works, He raises up some to speak and others to send, some to go, and others to give because you are His method. Being marked by generosity is deeply connected to your identity as a royal son or daughter of the Most High. It is a virtue we can all acquire and integrate into our lives.

~~~

The spiritual key which unlocks the promises and protection that come when you give is *Love*. When your heart is postured to love well, giving becomes effortless.

Action Steps

How to move past negative emotions that tithing may trigger in your life:

I would like to stand before you as a wife, a mother, and a daughter, and apologize for every single person who wounded you in the area of money. Moving past deep hurts starts with forgiveness. Do not hold them hostage for the pain they caused, but instead begin blessing them. This is a decision that may have to be made daily until the negative emotions are no longer present when the person or people come to mind. Simply saying, "I bless insert name and forgive them" will begin the healing process for your heart. Speaking a blessing over those who have hurt or offended you, whether you feel like it or not is a decision that will bring restoration to your life.

The Apostle Paul said, "Therefore, as God's chosen people, holy and dearly loved, clothe yourselves with compassion, kindness, humility, gentleness, and patience. Bear with each other and forgive one another if any of you has a grievance against someone. Forgive as the Lord forgave you. And over all these virtues **put on love,** which binds them all together in perfect unity" (Colossians 3:12-13 emphasis added).

How to start a God fund:

Open a separate checking or savings account and transfer over a percentage of your monthly income each month. The amount you decide to give is your personal decision and is between you and the Holy Spirit. Giving is about using the resources God has given you to further His Kingdom.

It is important to support our local churches but you are free to give to any ministry, mission, person or purpose you desire to help. The Apostle Paul writes, "Each one must give as he has decided in his heart, not reluctantly or under compulsion, for God loves a cheerful giver" (2 Corinthians 9:7).

How to open a 501-(c)(3):

It's a two-step process. The first step is state-level because you need to file articles of incorporation to become a nonprofit in your particular state. Your state's website will instruct you on the requirements needed specific to where you live.

The second step is filing a 1023-Form with the IRS which is the application to gain 501-(c)(3) status.[3] I recommend hiring a CPA to make sure it is done correctly and to ensure you stay in compliance each year.

Chapter Four

Saving and Investing

*I*t was 1986. My parents lived in Michigan and decided to leave the snow and the ice, take a leap of faith, and move to South Florida with three kids under the age of eight. My parents were both school teachers at the time and money was tight. In addition to having next to nothing in their savings account, my dad decided to pay off his father's debt. My paternal grandfather borrowed money from my mother's family to start a business and never paid her family back. To my dad's embarrassment, he decided to pay off the $25,000 loan his father owed, which was more than my parents combined yearly salaries at the time. With five mouths to feed, a loan to pay off, and a teacher's income that wasn't paying the bills, my dad decided to get his Series 7 and become a financial advisor. His decision to switch careers and enter into the world of finance would change the trajectory of my life. I grew up with financial stability and learned the value of saving, giving, and living below your means.

After being a commercial lender at Wachovia bank, I would eventually follow in my dad's footsteps, obtain my Series 7, and become a financial advisor. I learned there are a lot of good reasons to save and the majority of them fall into three buckets. Those three buckets are: emergency fund, children's fund, and an investment fund for building wealth. Let's go a little further into what each of those buckets are.

Bucket 1 | Emergency Fund

The first bucket is building an emergency fund that will cover 3 to 6 months of living expenses. Keep this sum of money in a savings account separate from your checking account. If you have to spend it at any point during an emergency, do your best to refill the account back up as quickly as possible. When a broken air conditioner, trip to the emergency room, a new transmission for your car, or even the loss of a job happens, having money set aside for unexpected emergencies will help you avoid credit card debt. Doing this also helps you sleep better at night by keeping stress levels low when those expenses occur.

There is a survey the Federal Reserve compiles on the economic wellbeing of American households every year. In their 2020 report, 39% of adults said if faced with an unexpected $400 expense, they would not be able to cover it with cash, savings, or a credit card charge that could be paid off quickly.[4] That is a sobering statistic and although we can't control the unexpected, we can prepare for it.

It's never too late to start your emergency fund with an automatic transfer of $100 or whatever else you can afford from your checking account into a savings account each month. Saving for your future is hard. Especially when you see your friends taking Instagram worthy vacations, never making a social media post in the same outfit twice, and carrying around expensive handbags. Skip the five dollar coffees five days a week and start an emergency fund. Your future self will thank you.

After your emergency fund is fully funded, it's time to save and prepare for the expected expenses in life by focusing on the next two buckets. A good rule of thumb is to budget 10% of your household income for saving and investing. If you are able to save more, then do it! From the amount you set aside to save and invest, figure out how much you can put into the children's fund and the investment fund. It will vary depending on your age, how many children you have, and your specific needs. For example, if your family is able to save $500 a month, it's up to you to decide how to allocate that money into the following two buckets.

Bucket 2 | Children's Fund

The second bucket is a savings fund that only applies if you have children or grandchildren. Out of the 10% you set aside for savings, put a portion of it into your children's fund. A study was done by the Lending Tree on the cost of a four year in-state public college. Their researchers found, on average, the cost is $25,290.00 which includes tuition, room and board, books, and transportation for four years.[5] Education is costly!

Saving for your child's college isn't impossible, it just takes foresight.

Prepaid College Savings Plans and 529 Plans

As of 2020, there are eleven states that offer prepaid college savings plans so check with your state's website to find out if you have this option. A prepaid college saving plan allows families to pre-pay for college tuition at today's rates versus what it would cost when your child attends. If you do not live in a state that offers pre-pay tuition or you are not absolutely certain your child will attend your in-state school, a 529 plan is a great alternative.

With a 529-plan, the money can be used for any college in any state. As soon as your baby or grand-baby has a Social Security number, they can become the beneficiary of a 529 account. It can be used for all types of higher education such as K-12 private schools, college, or graduate school. According to the IRS, contributions are considered gifts for tax purposes and the money grows tax deferred which means earnings are deferred from both state and federal tax. Some excellent news, when the money is withdrawn, it is tax free! If your child chooses not to attend college, you don't lose the money in the account.

Most 529 plans allow you to transfer the money to an eligible relative of the beneficiary. You read that right, you can transfer the money to an eligible relative. Eligible relatives include immediate family such as a sibling or parent, extended family like a niece or nephew, and even in-laws. While we are on the subject of relatives, my husband and I ask our family members to write checks to our kid's college funds instead of buying them birthday, Hanukkah, or Christmas gifts. This allows our family to take part in funding our kids education which in turn, helps to ease the burden off of us. If the money is withdrawn and you decide to use it for expenses not related to higher education, a penalty and income tax on profits incurred will be owed.

Uniform Transfers to Minors Act (UTMA) and Uniform Gifts to Minors Act (UGMA)

Some of you may be thinking, "I don't know if my child will utilize a college education fund and I am not interested in transferring the money to an eligible relative." If this is the case, a great savings alternative is the UTMA (Uniform Transfers to Minor Act) or UGMA (Uniform Gift to Minors Act). These are similar to a trust account but you, as the parent have full control and can withdraw money at any time for the minor's benefit. Once your child reaches the legal age of adulthood which is usually 18 or 21 years old depending on where you live, your child will have full access to the account. That means they can walk into the bank, show their driver's license, and withdraw the balance. Whether they start a rock and roll band with the money or decide to open a new business is totally out of your control. Since the money belongs 100% to them once they reach your states legal age of adulthood, they will have full access to it. If you are concerned about how your children might spend the money, refer to Chapter 8 which will help you teach them financial literacy and responsibility.

These accounts allow you to save, invest in the stock market, and even put real estate properties in the minor's name. The money can be used for any type of expense which gives you more flexibility than only being able to spend it on education. Keep in mind, the IRS requires a kiddie tax if there is unearned income over a certain amount so make sure your accountant is up to date on the rules. Should your income allow you to, saving money in an education fund and an UTMA or UGMA account is ideal. Imagine being able to pay for a four year in-state college and then topping it off by giving your child a funded savings account in their name when they graduate!

Bucket 3 | Investment Fund for Building Wealth

The third and final bucket is saving into an investment fund for building wealth. Although investing is generally correlated with retirement, it can be used for more purposes than that. The purpose of this portion of your savings is for retirement and for large purchases. Investments can be utilized for any type of purchase like a wedding, home, or car. It can also be put to use to start a new business, buy rental properties, leave as an inheritance to your children, etc. Everyone is going to have different individual goals with what they want to use their investments for. The one action investing will allow for is give you the ability to have buying power you wouldn't have had if the money wasn't invested through the years.

Investing is really about making informed decisions with your money with the goal of it multiplying for you. This takes time and does not happen overnight. When I say, it takes time, I am referring to 5,10, and in some cases, 20 years or more.

Managing your money and choosing to invest it wisely instead of it sitting on cash will pay off later in life. Understanding what the different financial tools are is important, but putting your knowledge into action and investing for your future is also imminent.

A lot of people in America are hoping social security is going to cover all their financial retirement needs. I am here to tell you, don't depend on the government for your retirement! Whatever Social Security is giving by the time you reach the qualifying age to receive benefits, consider it icing on the cake. The actual cake needs to be money you have saved and invested in assets. An asset is anything of value that can be converted into cash. Oftentimes, the focus is on minimizing expenses, thinking it will ensure enough money for retirement. Being frugal while having no savings in place is not a good financial plan. I'm not suggesting saving for retirement or for large purchases is easy to achieve, but the best things in life rarely are.

If you work 9am-5pm, chances are, you won't be able to hand your job down to your children or grandchildren. But you can leave them assets that produce income or convert to cash such as your retirement accounts, stocks, mutual funds, ETF's, bonds, real estate, etc. My goal in this section is to equip you with the understanding you need to feel comfortable and confident investing in assets for your future. Not every single investment in the open market is listed below, but I did include the most common investment vehicles so when you do decide to implement a financial plan for yourself or your family, you have the knowledge to make informed decisions.

Roth Individual Retirement Accounts (Roth IRA)

The most popular individual retirement accounts are traditional IRA's and Roth IRA's. Roth IRA's are my favorite, and a great way to save for retirement. Most banks have self directed retirement platforms so you can contribute monthly with no fees. The money contributed has already been taxed so the principal and earnings will be tax free when funds are withdrawn once you reach the qualified age set by the IRS. You can also withdraw contributions at any time without a penalty, but that only applies to the amount you've contributed to the account throughout the years, not the earnings.

Retirement accounts are regulated by the IRS so there are penalties if earnings are withdrawn early and there are limits on how much can be deposited each year. It's one of those accounts you put in "set and forget" mode until you are almost 60 years old. Depending on your filing status and income, the rules vary so check with your accountant before you establish a Roth IRA account.

Traditional Individual Retirement Accounts (IRA)

A traditional IRA account has advantages as well. Contributions can be taken as tax deductions in the tax year they are made. That means, the amount you add to the IRA account is a tax write off and the earnings are tax deferred. Regardless of which retirement account you choose, slow and steady wins the race when it comes to building wealth.

Example of long term investment:

Age: 23

Starting amount: $1,000

Monthly contributions: $200

Rate of return: 9%

Years to grow: Until 65 years old

This investment is worth: <u>$1,045,112.81</u> !

401(k) Plans

A 401(k) is a retirement plan sponsored by an employer. If the company you work for offers a 401(k) plan, it's another great tool to save for your retirement. You can invest a portion of your salary up to an annual limit set by the IRS and I encourage you to save the maximum allowed. Some employers will match the amount you save in your 401(k) so be sure to take advantage of that benefit, if matching is offered.

Stock Market

The stock market is a platform that allows individuals and institutions to buy and sell different types of securities that trade on the stock exchange. Stocks, ETF's, and mutual funds are the most commonly traded. When an investor makes a purchase, it provides capital to the company to grow and expand without having to borrow money from a bank. In turn, the investor gets to benefit from the profits as the company increases in value.

Example:

- I Love Coffee Company issues one million shares of stock at $10. It's a huge success and all the shares are sold.
- Doing this provides I Love Coffee with $10 million in cash flow (minus fees from the stock offering)
- One investor named Susan buys 500 shares, spending $5,000. Five years later, the stock is worth $15. This provides Susan, the investor, with a stock that is now worth $7,500. I Love Coffee Company was able to raise money and Susan was able to share in the profits over the years.

Example of a dividend payment from I Love Coffee:
$200,000 position at $100 a share
Annual dividend payment: $1.80 per share
Yearly dividends = $360 ($1.80 x 200 shares) or $30 a month

If you are a consumer of this product, the dividends paid annually could potentially cover your monthly coffee habit! You also have the option of reinvesting the dividend and buying more shares of the stock if you don't want to cash it out. I Love Coffee Company is an example and not all stocks offer dividends, but the ones that do offer it, are literally giving the investor some of the profits as a thank you for choosing to invest in their company and help them grow.

When it comes to stocks, dollar cost averaging is a great way to invest long term. Dollar cost averaging means you invest equal dollar amounts in the stock market at regular intervals of time such as monthly or quarterly, like $100 a month or $300 a quarter. Rather than trying to time the market, you buy in at a range of different price points throughout the year. Doing this helps give you a favorable average price for your investments.

If you are well versed in how stocks operate, feel comfortable doing your own research, and picking your own investments then self managing your money might be the most favorable avenue. As reported by Investopedia, the top three self directed online investment platforms for beginners are TD Ameritrade, E*Trade, and Merrill Edge.[6]

If you would rather hire a professional to get specific investment advice, like what stocks to buy, a licensed financial advisor or a certified financial planner (CFP) is the best way to go. The financial industry in the United States is highly regulated. This is a good thing for the consumer because it means there is a regulatory organization in place to oversee the industry. In order to become a financial advisor, a person needs to pass the Series 7 exam which tests they're understanding of topics on investment risk, debt instruments, options, taxation, equity, packaged securities, and retirement plans. In order to become a CFP, a person needs to pass the Series 7 as well as the certified financial planner exam. As reported by Investopedia, "Security professionals are regulated by the Financial Industry Regulatory Authority (FINRA), which administers the qualifying exams that professionals must pass to sell securities. FINRA also has the power to take disciplinary actions against registered individuals or firms that violate the industry's rules. The main benefit of FINRA is to protect investors from potential abuses and ensure ethical conduct within the financial industry."[7] The moral of the story is, don't get stock market advice from your neighbor, from your hairdresser, or from your mechanic. I am sure they are all wonderful and lovely people but when it comes to your hard earned money, do the research yourself or hire a financial professional!

Mutual Funds

Mutual funds are a group of investments like stocks, bonds, or other securities. Every mutual fund has multiple positions and has at least one professional fund manager. The fund manager buys and sells positions in the fund throughout the year, is in charge of diversifying the portfolio, and responsible for keeping it in line with the fund's investment objective. An example of an investment objective would be having a goal of diversifying risk and making a positive return for the fund holder.

The mutual fund world is big and there are a lot to choose from. Instead of only owning one stock or one bond, a person can own a mutual fund that has multiple stocks, bonds, or other investments in it. You can buy a mutual fund in just about any category. For example, if you love technology there are technology mutual funds that will have 20, 30, or even 100 different technology positions in their fund. If you love large, well known companies with household names, there are mutual funds designated to only investing in large companies. Whatever category you choose to invest in, the cost to purchase a mutual fund will vary. According to SmartAsset, on average, you can be expected to front a minimum of $2,500 to buy a mutual fund. However, there are funds that require amounts as little as $500. Because of this large difference in minimum investment amounts, it helps to shop around before selecting a mutual fund.[8] If you decide to purchase shares of a mutual fund, it is done at the close of the market because they are not traded throughout the day like a stock would be.

Exchange Traded Funds (ETF's)

Exchange Traded Funds (ETF's) are based on an index and for the majority, not managed by an actual human. An index tracks the performance of publicly traded companies and their stock prices. For example, the S&P 500 is an index that tracks the stock performance of 500 large companies. The purpose of an ETF is to mirror a specific index. If someone wanted to benefit from how the S&P 500 performed but did not want to buy all 500 stocks, they could buy an ETF which holds stocks that mirror the S&P 500. That particular ETF would rise and fall according to how the S&P 500 performed.

There are many ETF categories to choose from. As reported by Statistca, "As of 2019, there were 2,096 ETFs in the United States."[9] They usually have less internal fees than a mutual fund since it doesn't involve a professional fund manager. There is also no minimum, you simply buy an ETF share just like you would buy a stock throughout the trading day.

Bonds

Bonds are a type of fixed income. They are generally issued by the government, a municipality, or a corporation looking to raise money. For example, when an investor purchases a government bond, they are essentially lending money to the government. The money invested acts like a loan and in return, the issuer gives a fixed rate of interest to the buyer, typically, twice a year. Every bond will have a different maturity date, like 5, 10, or even 30 years. Once the bond matures, interest stops being paid and at that time, the investor receives their initial principal investment back.

Tax-free bonds are a popular type of bond, like a municipality, issued by the government. As the name indicates, the interest a person receives from the bond is exempt from tax regardless of the federal income tax bracket they fall into. Usually, these bonds don't mature for ten years or more so you can leave the principal amount as an inheritance to your children, if you choose to do so, while you live off the tax free interest.

Corporate bonds generally fall into two categories. The first is investment grade, meaning they have high credit which implies low risk. The second is speculative grade, meaning they have low credit which implies high risk. When a person owns stock in a corporation, they are considered a fractional owner of the corporation, but when an investor buys bonds issued by a corporation, they become lenders earning interest on their money. Not all corporate bonds are created equal, some have been nicknamed "junk bonds," so do your due diligence before purchasing.

A lot of people like to add bonds into their investment portfolio because of the steady stream of income it offers. They are not publicly traded like a stock so you have to purchase bonds from a broker. As reported by the Securities Industry and Financial Markets Association (SIFMA), the size of the worldwide bond market is over 100 trillion dollars![10]

Real Estate and Rental Property

If you would rather have a tangible asset that you can see and feel, real estate is an avenue for you to invest in. Proverbs 31:16 says, "She considers a field and buys it; out of her earnings she plants a vineyard." There is money to be made with land and the real estate that is built upon it. The goal is to own multiple properties that are residential, commercial, or both and rent the properties out to qualified tenants. After the mortgages are paid off, the monthly rent money from the tenants can be used as income to live on. And hopefully, the market values of the properties have increased as well. As with any type of investment, there is risk involved in real estate. If investing in real estate to build wealth excites you, there are numerous authors who have dedicated entire books on teaching the subject as well as online courses you can take. Become a student and learn as much as you can before choosing this as your investment path.

Watch It Grow

We live in a society that rewards instant gratification. Everywhere you look, experiences are offered with no delay whether it's two day shipping, streaming full seasons of your favorite TV show at once, or paying extra to skip the lines at amusement parks. Planning for your future and your children's future works a little different. It may not be instant but it is a meaningful pursuit that will fulfill the desires and goals set by you and your family. I encourage you to have a vision of what you want twenty-five years from now. Set aside any limited thinking or fear and close your eyes. Imagine things like the colleges your kids will go to, the weddings you will host, the family vacations you will take, the house you will retire in, the inheritance you will leave to your children, and anything else that comes to mind. These events can be accomplished with long term financial planning.

I understand each person reading this is not in the same stage of life. Some may be able to start funding all three buckets right away and others might only be able to start with the emergency fund. It's okay if you are not as far along as you want to be financially, but don't make excuses which keep you there for years on end. Saving month after month will enable you to gradually get to the finish line. Choose to make your long term financial needs a priority by paying yourself first. Meaning, the money you invest now will be used to pay your "future self" later in life.

All of the investments listed in this chapter have risk associated with them. Whether you decide to invest in real estate, bonds, the stock market, or all of the above, having a long term strategy using diversification and dollar cost averaging will help minimize the risk. It's never too late to put into motion an emergency fund, a children's fund, and an investment fund for building wealth. Start by funding one bucket at a time if doing all three at once seems overwhelming. The objective is to start!

~~~

The spiritual key which opens the door for you to achieve your financial goals is *Patience*. Proverbs 13:11 TPT says, "Wealth quickly gained is quickly wasted; easy come, easy go! But if you gradually gain wealth, you will watch it grow."

Action Steps

Which bucket should be prioritized first?

Your emergency fund should be the first bucket you prioritize. Next is the children's fund followed by the investment fund. If your income allows you to, consistently investing a certain amount in all three buckets each month is ideal. However, this is a general recommendation because depending on your current financial goals you may choose to change the order of buckets you fund and that's okay!

Do you need advice about financial investing and retirement?

It's important to have realistic goals for retirement. A financial advisor or certified financial planner will help lay out a detailed plan of how much you need to save each year and how many years you need to save to reach your specific goal. They will also guide you on what investments to make.

Research financial advisors and CFP's in your area and interview three before you make your choice. Banks such as Chase, Bank of America, WellsFargo, PNC, Citigroup, and local community banks provide in house financial advisors you can meet with. You do not have to hire someone at your bank but it's a good starting point. Make a list of questions before the meeting and share your goals with them.

How to open a prepaid college savings plan

or a 529 account:

As of 2021, The eleven states who offer prepaid college plans are Florida, Illinois, Maryland, Massachusetts, Michigan, Mississippi, Nevada, Pennsylvania, Texas, Virginia and Washington. Each eligible state has its own website which allows you to enroll your child in their prepaid college savings plan.

Most 529-plans are offered directly from the state you live in and in some states your yearly contributions can be used as a tax deduction. Each state has its own website which allows you to enroll your child in their 529-plan. You don't have to contribute to your state's plan. You can choose any plan you want, so it's worth comparing your options because there are many investment firms and financial advisors that offer 529-plans on their platforms as well.

How to open an UTMA or UGMA account for your child:

Your local bank representative or financial advisor can open an UTMA or UGMA account for you and help you choose the investments. Since your child is the beneficiary their social security number will be required. I recommend setting up monthly contributions into this account for the most favorable results.

Chapter Five

Debt

*D*ebt can sometimes bring on feelings of self judgement and regret but I am here to tell you, there is hope for you! This is a guilt free zone and my desire is for you to create an achievable plan and stick to it. Below you will learn how to lay out practical steps so you can start the journey of eliminating unwanted debt.

Borrowing Money

Is debt a sin? That's the million dollar question. Some people quote the scripture, "the borrower is a slave to the lender" (Proverbs 22:7) and others believe living completely debt free is so unattainable they give up altogether. In biblical times, if you did not pay back your lender, you contractually became their slave until your debt was paid off. Proverbs 22:7 mentioned above was literal. Fortunately for us, in the twentieth century, banks do not require you to become their slave or employee and work for free until your debt is paid. I do believe it is amazing to have absolutely no debt in your life and an honorable goal to achieve, especially when you reach retirement age. While the Bible does give warnings about borrowing money, it does not say you are out of the will of God or living in sin if you acquire debt. In some cases, like real estate and business expansion, borrowing money for the short term, like a year or less, can set you up to have a favorable outcome. It allows an individual or company to take advantage of opportunities that would otherwise be lost.

Loans have been around for centuries and are mentioned throughout scripture. In Matthew 5:42 Jesus says, "Give to the one who asks you, and do not turn away from the one who wants to borrow from you." In Exodus 22:25, God tells the Israelites, "If you lend money to My people, to the poor among you, you are not to act as a creditor to him; you shall not charge him interest." The banks in America and around the world are not as gracious as the Israelites were to their own people so we unfortunately have to pay interest on the loans we get. If you do receive a loan, plan to pay it off quicker than required which will limit the amount of interest paid out.

Debt is Not A Dirty Word

One of my first jobs in the financial industry was at a bank as a commercial lender. This meant I worked with business owners who applied for loans to purchase real estate, use as working capital, or for inventory and equipment. It was at this job I learned the value of using debt as a tool for growth. Many years later, I left the world of finance and entered into the fashion industry. I partnered up with a good friend and opened a high end women's boutique. A short time after opening, my business partner and I decided to move into a space that was double the size. The cost to expand was $50,000, but would give us the ability to have additional inventory and a custom build out. With this expansion we were able to add a denim bar, large shoe section, and over forty more brands which greatly enhanced the customer experience and kept us competitive. The first year in the larger space sales increased by 60% and maintained at that level year after year! The debt we acquired to expand was worth the reward. With the extra profit coming in, we were able to pay back all the money we owed in less than twelve months. In this case, the short term debt was beneficial in helping us reach our financial goals for the clothing boutique.

Long term debt like student loans and home mortgages can also be beneficial. Taking a loan to educate yourself that in turn creates opportunity for you to earn money and have a career is a positive decision. The same scenario applies to buying property. Having a mortgage to provide yourself or your family with a home gives you an asset that can increase in value over the years. Use wisdom when deciding what type of debt and how much debt is incurred. You don't want to over-leverage yourself. Over-leveraging occurs when too much money is borrowed resulting in the inability to pay interest and principal payments. Just because both the Old Testament and the New Testament do not call debt a sin does not mean you should buy a house above your means, obtain a business loan you won't be able to repay, or use your credit card irresponsibly. Psalm 37:21 says, "The wicked borrow and do not repay," so you have a moral obligation to repay debt. I encourage you to pursue what you can afford and count the cost.

Greed

Although the Bible does not say debt is a sin, it is very clear about calling greed a sin. The Apostle Paul says in Colossians 3:5, "Put to death, therefore, whatever belongs to your earthly nature: sexual immorality, impurity, lust, evil desires and greed, which is idolatry." If racking up debt is used to create an illusion of prosperity in your life then you are headed down the wrong path. When people get into situations where debt is used to have "bigger, better, and brighter" believing all of it equates to their value and importance, it is a symptom of something much deeper. The root problem of an insatiable desire to spend and accumulate is greed. Jesus said it plainly in Luke 11:39, "You Pharisees clean the outside of the cup and dish, but inside you are full of greed and wickedness." When money is used to portray a fake outward appearance of a flawless life, greed has entered in disguising itself as righteousness. There is a reason Apostle Paul warns us when he says, "The love of money is the root of all kinds of evil" (1 Timothy 6:10). One way to continually check the motives of your spending habits is always be willing to give. I did not say always give, I said always be willing to give. Doing this will protect you from building idols of greed in your heart.

Credit Cards

According to the Experian credit consumer review, the average American in 2019 had $6,194 in credit card debt.[11] That means each year credit card companies accrue on average, $991 in interest owed! Credit cards are not your enemy, but the interest accrued from keeping a balance is. Imagine someone handed you 9 one hundred dollar bills, 4 twenty dollar bills, a 10 dollar bill and a 1 dollar bill. Next, you were instructed to flush the $991 down the toilet. Sounds painful doesn't it? If you cannot keep a zero balance each month on your credit card by paying it off, then don't have one. If you currently have a past due balance on your credit card then stop using it until you can pay down the balance to zero.

Your credit card is not your emergency fund.

As mentioned in Chapter 4, I recommend building up an emergency fund that covers 3 to 6 months of expenses. Have this in place before opening a credit card. When you do charge items, follow a budget, use discernment, and keep a zero balance at the end of each month. There are benefits of a credit card like cash back, traveling for free with points earned, and building credit. Aside from your mortgage and student loans, the greatest use of debt is when it is short term.

Student Loans

If you already have a student loan the best advice I will give you is this — do not ever defer student loan payments. The reason it is a bad idea is because the interest accrued while you are not paying the student loan can double the amount of the original loan cost. That means, unpaid interest is added to the loan which will substantially increase the amount you owe. According to Forbes, student loan debt in 2020 is now at 1.56 trillion making the average student loan debt $32,731 and the average student loan payment $393 a month.[12] If you want to pay it off sooner, adding one or two extra payments a year will shorten the life of the loan.

If you do not have a student loan but are thinking of getting one to further your education and secure a solid job, be certain the degree you earn will translate into a career. There is nothing worse than a college graduate with an average of $30,000 of debt who can't find a decent job because the degree they picked isn't what companies need or want. As reported by the Career Cast, "On average, workers with a college education earn nearly twice those who only have a high school diploma. The top ten paying jobs straight out of college are investment banker, software developer, actuary, engineer, computer network administrator, internet marketer, financial analyst, pharmaceutical representative, web designer, and nurse."[13] This doesn't mean you have to pick a degree according to the list of top ten paying jobs. But definitely research which careers a degree will help you attain before you commit to getting a student loan.

Avalanche and Snowball Methods

Do you feel like you are up to your nose in debt? You might have credit card debt, student loans, car loans, and no savings, so perhaps you are feeling discouraged. You are not defeated! You can save for your emergency fund and put money towards paying down debt at the same time. It might take you a year or longer to fund your emergency account but the first step is to start! The length of time it takes will depend on how much you deposit each month and the total amount you are looking to save. Once the emergency fund reaches your goal amount, move that monthly savings towards your debt. For example, if you were putting $150 towards debt and $150 towards your emergency fund, now you can put the entire $300 towards debt payments. If you don't want to pay down your debt quicker and would rather move the monthly savings to another bucket like the children's fund or investment fund, that's okay too! Each person looking to pay off debt is going to have different financial needs and desires.

There are two beneficial methods for paying off debt. They are called the avalanche and the snowball method. Both methods involve making minimum payments on all debt each month. The avalanche method has you put your debt in order from highest to lowest interest rate. Debt with the highest interest rate is paid off first. Then, the remaining debt from the greatest to the least interest rate is paid off. Doing this will often save you the most money in interest payments over time.

The second way is the snowball method which involves paying off the smallest debts first before moving on to bigger ones. This method gives you quicker progress and helps keep motivation strong. Whether you choose one method over the other or do a combination of both, it's more important to start the journey then stressing over which method is more exemplary. Make a plan by writing out all your debts from the greatest amount to the least amount owed. Then, choose the avalanche or snowball method for the debts that have to be paid back in three years or less like your credit cards, car loans, medical bills, personal loans, etc. Once all of your short term debt is paid off, the amount that was set aside to pay off short term debt can now be used to pay off long term debt or put towards one of your savings buckets.

Mortgages

What is a mortgage? A mortgage is a fancy word used when a loan is taken out to buy a property such as a house or a townhouse. According to the US Census Bureau, the median home price in 2020 was $320,000.[14] The vast majority of Americans do not have this much cash on hand to purchase property which is why mortgage loans are so common. However, not all mortgage loans are created equal. For example, the interest rate can be fixed or adjustable and the terms, which is the length of the loan, can vary. Also, if you do not have 20% to put down, private mortgage insurance might be required by the lender.

The most favorable option is to choose a 15-year fixed rate loan instead of the typical 30-year loan. There are obvious advantages to doing this. Your loan gets paid off in half the amount of time which means you pay less interest and equity in the home is built much faster. The difference in payments made to the bank on a 30-year loan versus a 15-year loan can be hundreds of thousands of dollars. I am not exaggerating. Below is an example with easy math so you can understand further. For the sake of simplicity, I used the median home price mentioned above, a 20% down payment is assumed and principal and interest are included. Keep in mind, banks offer lower interest rates for 15-year loans.

Example of a $320,000 home with a 20% down payment:
$256,000 loan with 4% interest over 30 years ($1,222 a month) = $439,986 paid

$256,000 loan with 3.5% interest over 15 years ($1,830 a month) = $329,417 paid

The conclusion shows us that for the same exact house an extra $110,000 was spent over the life of the loan when a 30-year fixed rate was chosen. Ouch! Stick with a 15-year fixed rate mortgage to pay off your house quicker, it will bless your family for years to come. Doing this will also help you achieve a mortgage-free life by the time you reach retirement age.

Break-Even Scenario

If you are not planning on living in an area for the entire length of your loan, buying a house can still be a good idea. Some think renting is better if they don't plan on staying in one place longer than four or five years. The belief is, "I won't live in it long enough for the value of the home to increase, so why buy it?" If you buy a home and the value is the same when you decide to sell it, that is called a break even scenario. Using the monthly payment from the 15-year loan mentioned above, here is an example of a break-even scenario: You live in the home for 5 years and sell it for exactly what you paid for it. You know what that means? You lived rent free for 5 years. Say that with me one more time, rent free for 5 years.

Once you sell it, the mortgage balance you owe to the bank is paid off first, the remaining amount of money you receive covers the down payment you made along with all the monthly payments paid over the time you lived there. Simply put, you fronted a down payment to live somewhere and 5 years later got it all back. You might be thinking, "But I didn't make any money!" True! You also didn't lose any. I understand owning a home comes with extra expenses. Even if a few thousand dollars a year was spent updating and making repairs, you are still ahead of the game. Had you been paying rent for 5 years or 60 months at $1,830 a month (average 15-year loan payment) you would have paid out $109,800 and never seen it again. Break-even scenario doesn't seem so bad anymore, does it?

Buy Smart

When purchasing a home, do not become house poor. This means, do not buy a property that requires most of your monthly income leaving you with nothing to give or save. Just because you are approved to borrow a certain amount of money to purchase a home does not mean you should. Once you find out the mortgage amount you are approved for, ask what the monthly payments will be, including property taxes and homeowner's insurance, which is called a mortgage escrow payment. Annual property tax will differ from state to state but it is required. You will also need homeowner's insurance before a lender will issue a loan to you. A good rule of thumb is to make sure the monthly escrow amount and loan payment is 30% or less than your total net income each month. If it's not, buy a less expensive house because it's not worth it to live paycheck to paycheck while pretending to look rich!

Creating Extra Streams of Income

A solution which will speed up the process of paying down debt is creating extra streams of income. The income from a second job, whether home based or not, can be used specifically to pay off debt. The following ideas are to get your wheels turning and inspire you:

- We live in the age of the internet and with that comes home based jobs. More and more executives are hiring part time virtual assistants, research companies pay for online reviews, and companies like Upwork and Fiverr connect freelancers to end users for anything from graphic design, copy writing, and book editing. If you have administrative or creative design skills chances are you can be paid to do it from home.

- When was the last time you cleaned out your closets? A good standard to follow is if you have not worn it in a year then sell it! Poshmark, ThredUp, and The

RealReal are just a few of the online consignment stores with a high volume of web traffic to help your clothing sell.

- To all the artists reading this, Etsy is a great website that allows you to sell your handmade creations and gain exposure both domestically and internationally.

- Network marketing companies are another option, but steer clear if it requires a certain amount to be spent each month or a large upfront fee to join.

- Odd jobs like babysitting, cleaning houses, picking up part-time retail work during the holidays, delivering pizza, or becoming a Doordash driver on the weekends will also help bring in extra income.

Keep the Vision in Front of You

Paying off debt is not going to happen overnight. It may take a few years for you to pay off debt like credit cards, medical bills, or car loans. It is important to write down your goals and the vision you have for your life. Think about your "why" for getting rid of debt to stay motivated. If you need accountability then find some friends who are on the same journey and connect weekly to celebrate the wins and reset when there are setbacks.

~~~

The spiritual key which opens the door for you to pay off your debt is *Perseverance.* It will be hard work, but it will be worth it, so stay persistent!

Action Steps

Should you change a 30-year mortgage to a 15-year fixed rate loan?

The best time to attain a 15-year fixed rate loan is when you first purchase a property. If you currently have a 30-year mortgage then contact your mortgage broker and ask what is needed to refinance your mortgage to a 15-year fixed rate loan. Compare the numbers to see if it makes sense. The other option is to make one extra payment a year to pay it down quicker. Just making one extra payment a year makes a big difference. For example, if you have a 30-year mortgage and make an extra payment each year you will pay off the mortgage in 20 years instead of 30 years and save thousands in interest payments.

Were you taught to never get a credit card and should you open one?

I only recommend opening a credit card if you have atleast 3 months of expenses saved in an emergency fund. Once that is accomplished, as long as you can pay off your credit card balance each month then it's okay to open one. Doing this will establish credit since your credit score is a direct result of your debt being paid off on time. It's like a report card which shows you bought something and had the means to pay for it. In most cases, having a good credit score (above 700) will help you obtain a business loan or a mortgage at a favorable interest rate.

Is it possible to save in one of the three buckets and pay off debt at the same time?

Yes! First decide how much money you can set aside to pay off debt and to put away for savings each month. For example, if your budget for this is $500, decide how much of that goes towards savings and how much goes towards a debt payment. Once your debt is paid off, the entire amount that was set aside for both debt and savings can now be fully put towards the saving and investment accounts of your choice.

Chapter Six

Budgeting and Overcoming

*B*udgeting is when the rubber meets the road. Once you know how much money is coming in and how much is going out, you will gain freedom by making a plan. Some of the decisions you have to implement will feel really great and some may sting a little. Following through with a budget will help you face your current financial situation. Numbers don't lie and creating a budget will protect you from falling into the trap of avoidance, hoping spending problems will magically disappear. I promise you, there is clarity, growth, and great vision on the other side. You might not need to do it for the rest of your life but budgeting for a period of time, like a year, will teach you to be disciplined with spending.

The purpose of writing a budget is so you can be intentional about where your money is going. It is the practice of applying wisdom to your finances. Budgeting will also help minimize feelings of guilt when you do spend it on things that are not essentials. Feeling guilty for spending is the absolute worst and it establishes a negative association with money you don't want in your life. Think of a budget as a means to help you lower your stress and steward what God has given you. No matter how much or how little you have, your ability to steward money will directly impact your success in building wealth and maintaining it.

Budgeting Tips

If you are married, be sure to set goals together, but only assign one person the responsibility of managing the budget. A couple does not need two chefs in the kitchen sharing this responsibility. As long as you are both in agreement on what the budget needs to look like, one of you can take the role as the implementer. It can be the wife or the husband, preferably the spouse who doesn't have a tendency to spend all the time. Doing this will lessen financial tension in the marriage. Regardless of who is in charge of the budget, never hide money earned or money spent from your spouse. Lack of communication about household finances causes strife so once you are married, keep everything transparent.

If you are single, ask a trusted friend or family member to keep you accountable and help you stay on track with your budget. Schedule times to share and celebrate your financial wins with them and if you experience a setback, be quick to reach out for help and encouragement.

How to Write a Budget

The four steps in creating a budget:

1. Determine your income after you have paid your taxes. Your income before taxes is called your gross income and your income after you've paid your taxes is called your net income. Oftentimes, your employer will automatically pay your federal, social security, and Medicare taxes for you.

2. Calculate your expenses. A simple way to figure out your expenses is to check the recent transaction history on your bank account and credit cards. Then, put the expenses into categories. For example, living expenses would be rent or mortgage, utilities, and water. Transportation expenses would be car payments, car insurance, fuel, etc. You get the idea?

3. A general guideline is to spend 50% on essentials and allocate the other 50% to be spread across giving, savings, debt, and wants. Decide how much you can spend in each category based on your income after taxes. The following chart is an example and just a suggestion. Actual percentages assigned to each category will vary depending on your personal goals and financial situation.

Example Budget		Net Income $6,000.00
Essentials (50%)	Mortgage/rent, utilities, internet, cell phone, food, car maintenance, etc.	-$3000.00
Giving and Savings (20%)	Generosity, emergency fund, retirement, investments, etc.	-$1200.00
*Debt Payments (10%)	Student loan, car, motorcycle, dirt bike, boat, jet ski, etc.	-$600.00
Extra Curricular (10%)	Eating out, shopping, new clothes, etc.	-$600.00
Recreational and Fun (5%)	Date night, zoo, fairs, museums, vacations, etc.	-$300.00
Self Care	Facials, hair salon, nail salon, massage therapy, gym, etc.	-$300.00
		$0.00 left at the end of the month

*If you do not have debt, move this to another category!

The greatest way to track your progress is to download a budget app on your smartphone. According to NerdWallet, the best user friendly and free budgeting apps are Mint, PocketGuard, and Clarity Money.[15] Many people have also found success in using an Excel spreadsheet or the old fashioned pen and paper each month.

4. The goal at the end of each month is to have a zero balance after all the budget categories have been met. If there is money left over, it's up to you where the surplus is assigned to for the following month or for something in the future.

Spending less than you make is critical to your budgeting success. If spending less than you make seems impossible, consider two ideas. The first is, you may need to lower your expenses. The second is, you may need to earn more money. If that is the case, start looking for a better paying job that will allow you to earn more and reach your financial goals faster. Or, begin pursuing your dream of starting a business that will bring in more income.

Underearning

In some cases, the problem is not your expense category. You may have done your due diligence by cutting excess spending, canceling subscriptions you no longer use, and putting yourself on a tight food budget, but there is still not enough at the end of the month to pay your bills. If this is the case, you are underearning. Your time, knowledge, skills, and experience are worth something, so be sure you are being compensated accordingly. This might mean charging more for what you do, going back to school for more education, or a career change all together. If you do not have a college education or the idea of going back to school sounds daunting, there are many two-year programs that create a pathway for a six figure job once completed. For example, computer programming, radiation therapists, registered nurses, and dental hygienists are in the top ten careers for a two-year associates program.[16]

If you are stressed about getting student loans or spending the next two years taking night classes or online classes, an example that does not require a lot of upfront money or formal education is becoming a real estate agent. The point is, you are not stuck. Brainstorm with your spouse or close friends for career ideas because they know your strengths. You have control over the financial choices you make in your life and the career you choose. According to the Center for Disease Control (CDC), the average life expectancy in America is 80 years old.[17] This means, you have a lot more life to live and in the big picture, a few years of education to exponentially increase your income and quality of life is worth the sacrifice.

Financial Desert

Oftentimes, when a person sits down for the first time to write their budget and sees their income and expenses on paper, he or she can experience a myriad of emotions. Feeling overwhelmed, despair, or hopeless are very common, especially if a person realizes they are spending more than they earn and a real lifestyle change is needed. When this happens, a person may think a budget isn't going to help because he or she is in a financial desert with no hope of an end being in sight.

Life as a believer has mountain top experiences and valleys of hardships. The Apostle Paul said, "I know what it is to be in need, and I know what it is to have plenty. I have learned the secret of being content in any and every situation, whether well fed or hungry, whether living in plenty or in want. I can do all this through him who gives me strength" (Philippians 4:12-13). Of course, we all want to be living in plenty but there may be times in your life that you are in need.

In the Hebrew language, the word "midbar" has two meanings. The first meaning is "desert or wilderness" and the second meaning is "to speak." How profound that "to speak" and "wilderness" are the same word in Hebrew! If you have a history with the Lord are you really that surprised? God speaks to you in the wilderness so pay attention to what He is saying. Many heroes of the faith had their own desert experience. In the wilderness, God spoke to Abraham and gave him many remarkable promises, Moses received the ten commandments, David wrote numerous psalms, and John the Baptist was preparing the way for Christ. Even Jesus, before the start of His public ministry went into the wilderness for forty days. God uses circumstances to shape our character and build our spiritual muscles. Going through a financial desert does not have to be permanent but it will be used by God to build your faith muscles of trust. He wants you to prosper and be in health even as your soul prospers (3 John 1:2). Jesus will use everything you have been through in your life for His Glory. The trials and tests you endure will become your testimony. Getting on a budget, changing careers, going back to school — these all may be hard, these all might feel like a wilderness, but God will speak to you and be with you in those hard places.

God Your Redeemer

In the book of Ruth, we learn that Naomi, Ruth's mother-in-law, had a family member named Boaz who was extremely rich. Ruth's husband had died, which was Naomi's son, leaving no one to financially take care of her needs. Ruth could have gone back to her family and eventually married again but she chose to stay with her mother-in-law Naomi instead. Since Ruth was widowed and had no husband to provide for her, she asked if she could glean from the harvest at the fields owned by Boaz because Boaz was a close relative of Naomi (Ruth 2:1-2). After Ruth gained favor with Boaz, Naomi instructed her to lie down at his feet when he fell asleep on his threshing floor after eating and drinking. In the Jewish custom of that time, laying at the feet of a man indicated you wanted to be redeemed by that person. It was essentially a proposal of marriage. Boaz responded to Ruth by saying, "Do not fear, I will do for you all that you request" (Ruth 3:11). After Boaz made arrangements to redeem Ruth, the people at the gate of the city celebrated and said to him, "May you prosper and be famous in Bethlehem" (Ruth 4:11). These prophetic words would ring true in generations to come. Boaz and Ruth had a son named Obed, who was the father of Jesse, who was the father of King David. Not only was Ruth redeemed from a life of destitution as a widow, but Jesus came from the lineage of David, and Boaz would indeed be famous in Bethlehem because of his descendant Jesus who was born there and became the Savior of the world.

Boaz is a picture of Jesus who is your redeemer because you are redeemed through the blood of Christ (Ephesians 1:7). When you take your place at the feet of Jesus, He has the power to restore to you all that you have lost. Thus says the Lord, your Redeemer, The Holy One of Israel: "I am the Lord your God, who teaches you to profit, who leads you in the way you should go" (Isaiah 48:17). God will teach you to profit. He will lead you. He will redeem your finances.

Leaving the Wilderness

If you need to get out of a financial desert, ask Jesus to give you wisdom, clarity, and hope. God took the Israelites around Mount Sinai many times over the course of forty years because of their attitudes and mindsets. Moses said it should have only taken eleven days (Deuteronomy 1:2)! You don't need to walk around the same mountain in the wilderness for forty years in order to reach your promised land. Moses told the Israelites God would bring them out from under the yoke of the Egyptians, free them from being slaves, and redeem them with an outstretched arm and mighty acts (Exodus 6:6-7). And, all of it happened! The Israelites witnessed the impossibility of Pharaoh letting his work force, the Hebrews, leave the country (Exodus 12:31). Then, their finances were redeemed because they left with a plunder of silver, gold, and clothing given to them by their Egyptian masters (Exodus 12:35-36). If that wasn't enough, they saw incredible miracles, like the Red Sea parting, a cloud by day and a fire by night to lead them, manna rained down from heaven to eat, and water was provided from a rock. Even after experiencing all of those mighty acts, they still viewed themselves as Egyptian slaves and victims. But God saw them as overcomers, free, and redeemed.

Don't be like the Israelites in the time of Moses. Find out what He is trying to speak to you, surrender to it, and move onto the next season in your life. Not one person from the generation who was an Israelite slave in Egypt was allowed to set foot into the promised land, because of their mindsets (Deuteronomy 1:35). Their children, however, are the ones who entered the land. Before Joshua took the Israelites, who were permitted to go into the promised land, Moses told them, **"There does not need to be any poor people among you,** for in the land the Lord your God is giving you to possess as your inheritance, he will richly bless you" (Deuteronomy 15:4 emphasis added).

There are specific people for you to bless, places for you to go, and industries for you to influence. You have a destiny that you are meant to fulfill. The Holy Spirit is in the details and sometimes the answer is really practical but it usually takes letting go of control and trusting like you've never trusted before. Being disciplined to have a zero credit card balance, an emergency fund, a God fund, and saving accounts is hard. Approach God's throne of grace with confidence and ask for guidance so you may find the grace to help you in your time of need (Hebrews 4:16).

The purposes God has in His heart for you requires obedience on your part. Building a solid financial foundation in your life allows Jesus to give you keys to unlock doors He wants you to walk through. Ephesians 2:10 says, "For we are His workmanship, created in Christ Jesus for good works, which God prepared beforehand that we should walk in them." You are destined to make an impact in this generation. Sow good seeds of financial stewardship and watch as God moves mightily in your life to fulfill His purposes for you.

~~~

Once you are out of a financial wilderness (I pray it's sooner than later), the spiritual key you will need which unlocks the door for you to budget is *Self Control*.

Action Steps

Does budgeting make you feel trapped?

There is value in knowing how much money is coming in and how much is going out. Think of it like you are operating a business. Large corporations cannot succeed without proper and realistic budgets. Almost every decision made will be based on what the company allocated for each department. Your personal finances also need budget goals and structure. One way to stay motivated is to reward yourself when milestones are met. You can do this!

Are you underearning?

Ask God for wisdom because if any of us lack wisdom, we can ask for it and Jesus will give it generously without finding fault in us (James 1:5). Taking a personality test will help you become more self aware of your strengths and weaknesses. Myers-Briggs, the Enneagram, and Birkman are popular tests that can be taken online and offer a full explanation of your results. The second action you can take is to hire a life coach or find a mentor. They will assist you in identifying areas you excel in and keep you accountable to your professional goals.

Chapter Seven

Insurance and Estate Planning

*T*here are a lot of important people and items you want to protect in your life. For example, your family, home, vehicles, and health. You can protect them by purchasing various insurance policies and putting an estate plan in place. Some people have the belief God is in control and whatever happens, happens. Yes, God is sovereign but it is your responsibility to plan ahead to protect your family. When Joseph interpreted two dreams for Pharaoh, the king of Egypt, Joseph revealed to Pharaoh that his dreams meant there would be seven years of plenty and seven years of famine (Genesis 41:29-30). Because of this warning, one-fifth of the harvest was stored during the first seven years. Then, when the famine came, there was enough food for all the cities in Egypt and surrounding countries (Genesis 41:57) because a strategy was put in place during the years of plenty. They planned ahead and it paid off.

In Pharaoh's case, God was merciful and sent a warning so Pharaoh would have time to prepare his nation for the famine. Just like Pharaoh, I want you to be prepared for the unforeseen situations that may occur in your life. One way you can do this is by becoming familiar with the different types of insurance policies available to you, what they protect, and how to put an estate plan in place. Each is a wise and beneficial action to take for any person wanting to build wealth and protect that wealth.

Homeowner's and Renter's Insurance

In the United States, homeowner's insurance (HOI) is purchased to cover loss or damage to your personal residence. Most lenders, like banks and credit unions, will not issue a loan on your property unless you, the borrower, obtain HOI. The purpose of this insurance is to cover the cost of property damage in the event something unforeseen or negative happens. For example, a fire, hurricane, rain damage, vandalism, or a lightning strike. This insurance also includes liability coverage to protect you against lawsuits if a person injures themselves on your property.

The price of homeowner's insurance depends on the estimated cost to replace the property and the risk or liability level of the location of your home. HOI is considered a contract of indemnity which means it will put the insured back to the state they were in prior to the loss. If you answer yes to any of the following questions, your HOI coverage may cost more because of the risk associated with the location of the property.

- Is your property located on a flood plain?
- Is your property across the street from the ocean?
- Is your property near a fault line?
- Is your property near a dry forest?
- Does your property have a lake, river, or retention pond on it?

Renter's insurance (RI) is used to protect the owner of the property if the person renting damages the premise. It is also used to cover unexpected events such as theft, damage to the renter's belongings, or reimbursement for hotel bills if the rental becomes uninhabitable. Many landlords include a requirement in their lease that renters obtain RI before they can move in. It does not insure replacing the dwelling, which makes RI significantly less expensive than a homeowner's insurance policy.

Auto Insurance

It is common to think the only purpose for auto insurance is to replace car parts that are damaged in a car accident or replace the car altogether if it is totaled. This is true, but there are more benefits it offers than just a needed replacement.

Auto Coverage Examples:
- Rental Reimbursement Coverage: This coverage is optional but it's nice to have if your car is being repaired

from an accident because it will reimburse you for the money spent on renting a car.

- Comprehensive Coverage: This coverage will pay to repair or replace your vehicle if it's stolen or damaged.
- Collision Coverage: If you have a loan or a lease on your car this is required by your lender. If your car is paid off, it's optional. The purpose of this coverage is to protect your vehicle from a collision with another car or an object (like a fence). Not to be mistaken with liability coverage which pays for the damage of another person's car.
- Uninsured Motorist Coverage: This is required in some states and I recommend having the maximum amount you can get even if it's not mandatory. It protects you when a car accident takes place and the other driver has no insurance.
- Liability Coverage: It helps pay for two things and is required in most states. The first is to repair another person's property (like their car) if damage occurs. The second is bodily injury liability which covers the medical bills if you are found responsible for causing the injuries. Each of these have "liability limits" which is the maximum amount the insurance company will pay out.

Example From Allstate Insurance Company:
You are at fault for a crash that injured three people in another car. Your bodily injury liability limit per person is $50,000 and your bodily injury limit per accident is $100,000. If Person 1's medical bills total $40,000, Person 2's cost

$30,000 and Person 3's cost $25,000, you're likely covered. Each person's bills were under $50,000 (your bodily injury limit per person), and the total cost of injuries is $95,000, which is lower than your $100,000 bodily injury limit for a single accident.

But suppose all three people had $50,000 in medical bills, totaling $150,000. In that case, your bodily injury liability coverage would pay $100,000 toward those bills, and **you may need to cover the remaining $50,000 yourself**. [18]

My advice regarding auto insurance is to have enough coverage so you do not ever need to come out of pocket for expenses. This might mean having more coverage than what your state requires. It's worth making a phone call to your insurance agent and looking into it.

Umbrella Insurance

Umbrella insurance acts like an umbrella on a rainy day. It is extra insurance which covers unforeseen lawsuits or expensive claims that exceed the amount of coverage you have with your other standard policies. It has to be purchased as an add-on to an existing policy like your homeowner's insurance or auto insurance. No one wants to think about being in a nasty lawsuit but umbrella insurance will come to your rescue and cover the attorney's cost and the amount you are being sued for. (There are some things it won't cover like criminal acts or flood damage).

A lot of people think if they have no money it doesn't matter if they get sued because the opposing party would not be able to collect anything. Depending on which state you live in that may not be the case. Some states allow for wages to be garnished from lawsuits. Meaning, a portion of your paycheck will be automatically withdrawn until the debt you owe is paid in full.

A lawsuit will most likely financially disrupt your life and umbrella insurance is an affordable way to shield your finances. According to the Insurance Information Institute, you can buy a $1 million personal umbrella liability policy for about $150 to $300 per year.[19] That's as little as $12.50 to $25 a month!

Health Insurance

Health insurance typically covers medical costs, prescription medications, surgeries and in some cases, dental and vision. Large corporations generally offer an employee sponsored plan at an affordable price. If you are self-employed be sure to hire an insurance agent to shop the market for the best rates and fair coverage because sometimes a share plan like Medi-Share or Liberty-HealthShare end up making the most sense.

Terms to be familiar with:
- Premium: The amount paid every month for health insurance coverage.
- Deductible: The amount paid out of pocket before the insurance starts to cover expenses.
- Co-pay: The fixed amount paid out of pocket for a medical related visit or prescriptions.

- Co-insurance: The percentage paid out of pocket for a medical related visit.
- Out of pocket maximum: The maximum you will spend out of pocket for medical care. Insurance companies have to pay 100% of medical expenses if this is met. The maximum amount will vary depending on what type of health insurance plan you have.
- Health Savings Account: Allows you to contribute monthly to a savings account with the sole purpose of paying for health care costs. As of 2020, you can contribute up to $3,550 for self-only coverage and up to $7,100 for family coverage. The funds roll over year to year if you don't spend them and can earn interest or other earnings, which are not taxable.[20]
- Medicaid: Government run health insurance program only available to low income individuals who meet certain criteria.
- Medicare: Government run health insurance program for people ages 65 and older and for qualified younger people with a disability.

Health insurance can get pricey but it might end up being more expensive if you don't have it. Medical Bankruptcy is still common even with the Affordable Care Act. According to a recent study, more than half of all bankruptcies (58%) can be tied back to medical expenses and an estimated 530,000 families in America file for bankruptcy each year because of medical bills and health issues.[21] Having the right health insurance in place for you and your family will provide you with much needed financial protection.

Long-Term Care Insurance

Do you have a grandparent that lives in a nursing home or has a paid caregiver come to their house to help with daily tasks? Have you ever wondered where the money came from to make that possible? The American Association for Long-Term Care Insurance reported that people older than 70 file more than 95 percent of long-term care insurance claims, and nearly 7 in 10 claims are filed after age 81.[22] Long-Term Care insurance (LTC) covers the cost of a nursing home, assisted living facility, or in-home care which are expenses not paid for by Medicare or health insurance.

The burden of this expense will end up on the shoulders of family members if LTC is not put in place. Most financial advisors say the best time to purchase a long-term care policy, assuming you're still in good health, is between the ages of 60 and 65.

Long-Term Disability Insurance

Do you know anyone who couldn't work because of an injury? Long-term disability insurance provides money if a medical situation happens that prevents you from working for three months or more. It will cover anywhere from 40-60% of your salary and last up to five years depending on the policy you purchase. Most companies offer it to their employees which is great. If you do not work for a company that offers it, you can purchase an individual policy. Keep in mind, this type of insurance is not to make you rich, it is designed to cover a portion of your income in the event you are physically unable to do your job.

Short-Term Disability Insurance

Short-term disability insurance is a type of protection for a temporary injury, illness, or even for post-pregnancy. For example, it can be used for a flight attendant who needs time off from hip surgery or a teacher needing time off to recover from cancer treatments. Another popular use is for women who work at companies that do not offer paid maternity leave. It can cover part of your income while out of work due to the birth of a child. Depending on the policy you choose, purchasing short term disability insurance will typically cover 60% of lost wages and generally last six months.

Identity Theft Protection

The purpose of identity theft protection is to protect your personal information because if it is used in a fraudulent way it can cause major financial losses. A thief can steal your social security number, date of birth, address, debit and credit card numbers and more. According to the Department of Justice, in 2016, 10% of Americans over the age of 16 became victims of identity theft.[23] There are a number of companies you can hire for identity theft protection that will monitor, protect, and reimburse you. US news reported the top three identity theft companies of 2020 were IdentityForce, IdentityGuard, and PrivacyGuard.[24]

Estate Planning

Estate planning isn't just for the ultra wealthy. I encourage you to start with what you can afford. For the majority of families, obtaining term life insurance and putting a will in place or establishing a living trust is all you will need to do. You can always expand on your estate planning as your needs and financial status change.

If you are married, have one or more children, are in the age range of 20-45 and the main income producer, then term life insurance is an affordable way to provide financial protection for your estate. The purpose of term life insurance is to leave the immediate family with a sum of money to ease the burden of expenses when the income producing spouse is deceased. Although this insurance product is not a savings account, the money a beneficiary receives from it mirrors one. According to ValuePenguin, in 2020 the average monthly rates from the top five largest life insurance companies for a 30 year old healthy male who was looking to purchase a 20-year term policy with a $500,000 death benefit was only $26.20 a month.[25]

A safety net was installed when the Golden Gate Bridge was being built in Northern California. This was done in the event a worker fell from its vast height topping out at 746 feet. There were 19 iron workers who lived after they fell and their families are grateful to this day for that net. Term life insurance is your safety net. You may or may not need it but in the rare chance you do, you will be grateful to have it.

In addition to term life insurance, a will is very important to have. The purpose of a will is to state your final wishes and give instructions on who you want inheriting your assets and belongings. It can also appoint guardians for minor children. Keep in mind, every written will is required to go through probate. Probate is the legal process in the state you live in when the written will of a family member is validated in court after their death. Once the will is authorized by a judge, the named executor can carry out the requested responsibilities that were listed in the will. The process ensures the deceased person's debts are paid off first and after that, the remaining assets are given to the correct beneficiaries. Not everything you own has to go through probate. Things like retirement accounts, life insurance policies, and property that is jointly owned will bypass probate and transfer directly to the beneficiary with proof of a death certificate. If a beneficiary is not named, the courts will require the probate process so make sure you have named beneficiaries on all your assets that allow for it!

Another layer of protection is a living trust which should only be drafted by an experienced estate planning attorney. The main purpose of a living trust is to avoid probate and leave a lasting legacy. The reason people want to avoid probate is because it can be time consuming and there is an expense associated with it. Sometimes court fees or attorney fees end up cutting into the heir's inheritance. If you have a living trust, items and assets are owned by the trust and not the person who died, which means it does not need to be handled through the probate court. Instead, a trustee is appointed, like a trusted family member or a financial advisor to carry out your wishes. Just about anything can be named in a living trust. Some examples include vehicles, jewelry, furniture, bank accounts, and real estate. Instead of John Smith owning a car or a house, John Smith Living Trust owns them. In order to fund the living trust, the deed of the property and the title to the vehicle would have to be transferred into the name of the trust. A living trust can be revocable or irrevocable based on your specifications. A revocable trust can be changed or terminated during your lifetime. On the contrary, an irrevocable trust means it cannot be changed during your lifetime or after your death. The most common trust is irrevocable but your estate planning attorney will help you make the best decision based on your individual wishes.

Aside from avoiding probate, the one major difference between a living trust and a will is conditions. In a living trust, you can list conditions that have to be met before a beneficiary receives the items or assets. Some people refer to this as, "controlling your money from the grave." For example, requiring your grandchild to finish a four-year college in order to inherit your vintage car, stocks, or diamond jewelry is something a living trust can include. Whether or not having a living trust makes financial sense for you, everyone needs a will. An attorney can write a will for you or you can do it yourself online. As reported by Investopedia, the top three websites that offer online will making services are Nolo's WillMaker and Trust, US Legal Wills, and Trust & Will.[26]

The goal of having insurance products and estate planning in place is to safeguard yourself and your family. I give my kids vitamin C and elderberry every single day. Doing this will not stop them from catching something and getting sick, but they will recover quicker because I have put forth preventative measures to strengthen their immunity. Insurance and estate planning work the same way. They don't guarantee negative situations won't happen but if they do, the process to deal with it becomes a lot less stressful.

~~~

Action Steps

What are your options if you can't afford health insurance?

If you qualify, Medicaid is a government run program for low income families that will help cover your medical costs. The Department of Health and Human Resources lay out the guidelines.[27] Another option is to go to walk in clinics. Many of them offer monthly membership programs with affordable flat rate pricing and reduced office visit fees for individuals and families. Research your specific area to find out what your city has to offer. Something is better than nothing, so weigh out your options before you completely rule out having some type of medical coverage.

How much term life insurance do you need and who do you call for a quote?

A local insurance agent like the one you hired to provide you with car insurance or a financial advisor will advise you on how much coverage you should obtain. There are also insurance companies with online platforms that will allow you to apply on their websites. NerdWallet reported the top three life insurance companies of 2020 were Northwestern Mutual, Haven, and MassMutual.[28]

Where can you buy a long term care or long term disability insurance policy?

An insurance agent or financial advisor can walk you through the steps of obtaining a long term care or long term disability insurance policy. In 1996 the Health Insurance Portability and Accountability Act (HIPAA) was passed standardizing all of the long term care insurance policies. This means all LTC policies are required to have the same contractual requirements and benefits. On the contrary, the benefits of a long term disability insurance policy will differ depending on how much coverage you choose.

Chapter Eight

Teach Your Children

H aving children is like getting a clean slate in life. It is the hardest, yet most rewarding experience to raise a human being. In their younger years you are responsible for making the majority of their financial decisions. The sobering reality is, every parent will be held accountable before the Lord for how they stewarded their child's early life. The encouraging news is, all the things you wish someone taught you about money, you can now teach your kids! Money mindsets and habits are a learned behavior. Being transparent with your children and teaching them the fundamentals of how money works is crucial for the following reasons:

1. Eliminates fear about the subject
2. Builds confidence in their ability to manage money
3. Sets them up for financial success

Do not rely on the school system or the church to teach your children about finances because it is your responsibility as their parent to do it. Giving, saving, and the impact of debt are topics you can coach your kids in. The Nasdaq reported 70% of wealth is lost in the second generation because the second generation who received the money were not educated and equipped to steward the wealth once they inherited it.[29] We must do better as parents. Teaching financial knowledge and then showing them how to apply the wisdom is the best way for your children to learn. Proverbs 24:3 says, "Through wisdom a house is built, and by understanding it is established. Through knowledge its rooms are filled with rare and beautiful treasures."

The goal is to give your children a better financial foundation than what you had, so they are set up for success. A good person leaves an inheritance for their children's children (Proverbs 13:22) and when most people think of an inheritance, money probably comes to mind. However, the definition has more meaning to it than just money. The Merriam Webster dictionary defines an inheritance as: possessions, property, and traditions. Traditions are a belief system about information that is handed down to the next generation.[30] An inheritance to your children is not only about leaving them physical money or assets, it includes teaching them about it too!

Use Your Words Wisely

Jesus upped the ante when He said in Matthew 12:36-37, "But I tell you that everyone will have to give account on the day of judgment for every empty word they have spoken. For by your words you will be acquitted, and by your words you will be condemned." Anyone else feel convicted after reading that?... me too.

The words you speak about money matter.

The phrase "we can't afford it" needs to leave your vocabulary. Children should never carry the financial burden of their parents. Never. If there is stress and tension around money in the home, they will associate anxiety with it and seeds of fear will be planted. If your kids want something and you don't want to spend money on it then simply tell them, we are using our money for other things like your soccer equipment, going out to eat as a family, your dance class, your sibling's car, or something that relates to your circumstance.

Teach them that you do have money and you are in charge of choosing where it is spent. The reality is, *you can afford things*, it is a matter of what you are choosing to afford. This will squash the poverty mindset that you do not want to instill in your children. It will also leave space for them to feel comfortable coming to you when they have financial needs at school or for personal items. Create an environment in your home where you can have open communication with your children about making choices with money. Doing this will allow your children to feel safe and know a plan is in place. Psalm 37:25-26 says, "I was young and now I am old, yet I have never seen the righteous forsaken or their children begging bread. They are always generous and lend freely; their children will be a blessing."

With the help of the Holy Spirit, let your words be like choice silver (Proverbs 10:20) and your lips feed and guide your family. Let no unwholesome talk come from your mouth, but only what is helpful for building others up in your family according to their needs (Ephesians 4:29).

Bags of Gold

In the parable of the bags of gold, Jesus tells a story to his disciples on the Mount of Olives. The story was about a businessman who left on a long journey and gave three of his servant's bags of gold to invest for him while he was away. The first servant was given five bags of gold and doubled the money to ten bags. The second servant was given two bags of gold and doubled the money to four bags. The third servant was given one bag of gold but was afraid of making a mistake so he decided to bury it (Matthew 25:14-30). It is a lesson about using the skills and abilities God has given us to further His kingdom. However, the particular talent Jesus refers to in this parable is bags of gold, or material wealth, so it is paramount not to overlook that.

In this parable, fear largely influences the actions of the third servant. Why was he afraid and who taught him to feel insecure about his ability to manage money? Most people are afraid of what they do not know. So, teach your children the principles of how money works and its purpose so they have nothing to fear. The more your children understand about money, the more success they will have as a good steward of it. The words you speak surrounding money will shape your children's fundamental belief system about it which will determine their attitude and ultimately their actions concerning it.

Core Responsibilities and an Allowance System

I am a big believer in children having core responsibilities and an allowance system. An example of a child having a core responsibility is making their bed, cleaning up toys after using them, putting away the dishes, taking out the trash, and anything else that helps keep order in your house. Requiring them to have core responsibilities lays the groundwork for a heart that is willing to serve and give while getting nothing materialistic or monetary in return.

On the other hand, an allowance system is putting a financial reward structure in place which is beneficial for tasks that are not core responsibilities. Sometimes children need a little motivation to accomplish activities they weren't otherwise interested in doing. An example would be to give a dollar amount when they finish reading a book that isn't required for school or for every "A" they earn on their report card. Another example is to give them money when a chore is done like cleaning your car or mowing the lawn. Giving an allowance helps your kids understand the value of money. It also encourages them to save which allows them to learn what it is like to wait in order to buy something that has a larger value. The payments you give don't have to be every time something is done. Instead, you can tally up what was accomplished and pay them in one lump sum bi-weekly or monthly.

It is up to you to determine what the core responsibilities are and which activities qualify for an allowance. You can play a powerful role in teaching your children the value of work and receiving a reward through an allowance system. You can be the first "boss" they are accountable to while teaching them the basics of what it means to earn money.

Matching Funds and Saving

When I was fourteen years old, my dad told me he would match the amount of money I saved in order for me to purchase my first car. I started babysitting and got a job as a hostess at a local deli. I saved every dollar I made for two years because I was determined to get a car when I turned sixteen years old. With the matching funds from my parents, I was able to buy a blue Mitsubishi Eclipse and her name was Princess. Owning a car which was paid for with my own money gave me a sense of responsibility and I took a lot of pride in taking care of it.

Matching funds can be used for anything, it does not have to be a big purchase. If your son or daughter isn't old enough to have a job then any money received for their birthday or the holidays can be matched. If you have a financial reward system in place for tasks that are not core responsibilities then that money can be matched as well. Matching funds will motivate your children to save. It also allows them to experience the reward of being able to purchase items they earned with their own money. Cultivating this type of positive reinforcement will provide them with a healthy foundation for saving. And let's be honest, it also encourages your kids to have an attitude of gratefulness for their possessions instead of feeling entitled.

Some parents don't want their kids getting a job until after they turn eighteen or after they graduate college because they want all their focus to be on academics, sports, music, etc.

I completely understand the importance of a child excelling in a certain area especially if it opens doors for them to receive scholarships to further their education. However, there will come a time for your child to leave your house and start their career. By now they are between the ages of 18 to 23 and instead of you being responsible for almost all the financial decisions made in their life, they are.

Once they start earning money, whether it's from an allowance or a job, I suggest you go with them to the bank and open a savings and checking account in their name. Teach your children how a checking account functions and strongly advise them to set up an automatic transfer from their checking account to allow a percentage, like 10%, to go into their savings account each month. Doing this will give your children an early start to save for emergencies, large purchases, and investments.

Thankfulness and Giving

Thankfulness is something we all want embedded into our children. It is better to teach them thankfulness for what they do have instead of focusing on what they can't have. A practical way to teach thankfulness and giving is to ask your child to choose one gift received from their birthday or from a holiday. Then, have them give it away to a foster care home, orphanage, or a child in need. It allows your children to see there is a big world out there with a lot of people who are in a disadvantaged position. It also encourages them to be thankful for what they do have and help those who have less. There is a reason they don't come out of the womb knowing how to share! Children have to be taught to give and shown the value it adds to the lives of others. Explain the reasons behind the giving and involve them in the process. Acknowledge it can be hard but also praise them for doing it. When they see your approval and how proud you are of their actions, it will become easier.

Children first learn what giving is from adults and it's usually their parents. You are the model influencing their attitude about it. You do not have to tell them all the times you give financially but it is worth teaching them how their giving makes an impact.

There are so many ministries and charities to give to so find out what your child is passionate about and show them how they can financially make a difference. The following are just a few examples to get you thinking about where to give.

- Giving to your local church which in turn supports single mothers, widows, and feeds the poor
- Giving to ministries that are saving children from the grips of sex trafficking
- Giving to special needs ministries
- Giving to foster care homes
- Sponsoring children who need meals in the United States or internationally

The list goes on and on with the impact your children can make by giving. There are so many things they can give to that will change history. Consider your child a lobbyist for God. What will they stand for? What will they help finance which will affect their generation and the next?

If your children are receiving money from an allowance or a job, a percentage of it can be set aside into a God fund or piggy bank as their tithe. After it builds up to fifty dollars (or another agreed upon amount), have them choose a charity, a missions organization, a church, or someone in need to give the money to. Using this type of positive reinforcement will help build a strong giving muscle in them. Once adulthood is reached and a career is obtained, giving a percentage of their income away will be second nature. By involving your children in the giving process during their developmental years, you are setting them up for spiritual success.

Spending

The best way to teach your kids about spending, is to let them spend! It's important they learn what things cost. If they are mature enough, give them the freedom to take charge of the shopping list at the grocery store so they can start to learn the expense of feeding a family. Once they turn 16, open a credit card in their name with a $500 limit. Only let them make small charges on it, like their cell phone or gas for their car. Teach them to pay off the balance each month and the benefits of doing so. This will establish credit in their name and it allows them to learn how to be wise with debt. If you are comfortable with your child getting a job and earning their own money, 16 is the perfect age for them to begin working. It is so necessary to learn the principles of smart spending, especially during the teenage years.

Mission Trips and Gratefulness

Encouraging your kids to take a mission trip outside of the United States will increase their gratefulness for what they have access to in everyday life. Most mission trips require money to be raised in order to go. That means your child will learn what it is like to be on the receiving end of someone who is raising money. Chances are, once they attend a mission trip and see the impact it makes, they will probably be generous in helping others go on trips as well.

Shortly after I graduated college, I went to Bolivia on a mission trip with a group from my local church to help an orphanage. It was eye-opening to see the level of poverty the children and adults were experiencing. We were able to paint and renovate the facility, which allowed for extra beds, and of course, we played with the orphans who were living there. On the trip I was able to serve, give, and understand how extremely grateful I should be for my life in America. Some of us were told to finish our plate of food when we were young because "kids are starving in China," and it probably went in one ear and out the other. But to experience what it is like in an underdeveloped country firsthand— to see it with your eyes and feel it with your senses is, I believe, the most effective way to appreciate your everyday blessings.

Contentment

Teaching contentment is a hard subject for children and adults. Kids observe everything, especially what other friends own or what activities they are doing. If you are reading this and you have kids, then you know comparison is a large part of the way they process feelings about the things they want. Can you recall a time when your son or daughter asked for a new toy because their friend had it? Or the newer version of their cell phone because they felt it would keep up their status of being "cool?"

In our consumer-driven culture, teaching contentment can be challenging but it is possible. I suggest three ideas to help you guide your kids. First, be their example. If they see you are grateful and at peace, they will be grateful. Show your children how to be happy for others and assure them they are exactly where God wants them to be—in your family! Second, limit commercials. Whatever those ads are selling, they are not going to bring fulfillment. Finally, have discussions about comparison with your kids. Chances are they will be exposed to social media at some point if they aren't already. The subtle messages given on social media can influence the way your children think about themselves. You are the voice meant to shape their identity, and no amount of likes or new outfits will accomplish that.

Dreaming Big

Let's dream big. As a parent, if you made a list of all the major financial things you could provide for your children from birth to adulthood what would it look like? Think about what you can financially do for them that was done for you which made a positive impact. And, think about what was not done monetarily for you that you would like to provide for your children. Some ideas might include matching funds for their first car, paying for a four year college education, buying property in their name as their first rental investment, paying for a wedding, giving a down payment on their first home, providing a night nurse when they have their first baby, etc. You are their first example of what it means to be provided for. It will directly influence their view of God as their provider until they are emotionally mature enough to know the difference.

The dreams you have to financially bless your children can be accomplished! In chapter 4 on saving and investing, I referenced two ways to help those dreams happen. The first idea is to have a separate savings account with investments, like stocks or ETF's, that can be cashed out for large purchases. This is the account to save money in, in order to fund dream gifts like a wedding or a down payment for their first home. The second idea is an education fund or an UTMA account. The education fund will keep you on track for covering some or all of their college education. The UTMA account will give them a lump sum of money or assets when they reach adulthood.

Example of an Education fund:
Starting amount: $1,000
Monthly contributions: $100 (set it and forget it)
Rate of return: 9%
Years to Grow: 18
In 18 years, this investment will be worth: $58,658

It is never too late to start saving for your children and something is better than nothing. Make them a priority because they are the future!

Good Stewards

I firmly believe if Jesus can trust us with money, He can trust us with anything. We need a generation that can be trusted with more and it is our job to teach our children to steward money well. In the parable of the gold bags mentioned earlier in this chapter, the first two stewards doubled the businessman's money. His response to both of them was exactly the same even though they were given different amounts to invest. He said, "Well done, good and faithful servant! You have been faithful with a few things; I will put you in charge of many things. Come and share your master's happiness" (Matthew 25:21 & 23)! Sometimes our focus is too heavily weighted on what we have or what we believe we don't have. Kingdom economics shows us it is more important to teach our children to focus on *what they do* with what they have.

For the mothers reading this, not only did God form your children in your womb, there is also a book written about your child's life. Psalm 139:16 says, "Your eyes saw my unformed body; **all the days ordained for me were written in your book** before one of them came to be" (emphasis added). There is a book written about your child's life filled with promises from God and a destiny for them to live out. Be the catalyst to allow them the freedom to fulfill their purposes on earth.

Money should never be a reason your children don't step out in faith for the things God ordained them to do. You were created to parent the children God gave you. You were made for them. You are raising the next generation of lawyers, bankers, government officials, doctors, teachers, ministers, musicians, actors, artists, authors, etc. It's not about you. It's about your little humans who will grow up to be adults who will influence and shape this world. Teach them the ways of God!

Tent Pegs

You have a sphere of influence or what I call, tent pegs. It's the size of the tent God has entrusted you with and how much impact you have in the lives of those around you. It might be the business you own, the children you are raising, your friends, or the people at your workplace. There are a lot of things in life you can't control, but the one area you do have a voice in is your influence. Just because the leaders in the country you live in or the boss at the company you work for have a different set of values than you, does not mean your household has to follow it.

Your children will learn character and what their moral compass is from you. You can teach them to fear the Lord and to shun evil. In the words of Joshua, "But as for me and my household, we will serve the Lord" (Joshua 24:15). Joseph, David, Elijah, Daniel, Nehemiah, and others all had leaders who did not desire to serve the God of Israel. But you know what? These men of God were still used mightily by the Spirit of the Lord to shape their society. In the same way, your children can be God's method. Steward the children God has given you to be a light and live out biblical standards instead of what the world expects from them.

Proverbs 22:6 instructs us to train up a child in the way they should go and when they get older, they won't depart from it. Parenthood is a ministry, so ask the Holy Spirit to help you teach your kids about finance. Pray for them to understand and speak with wisdom on the subject. By doing so you are creating an atmosphere for your kids to have a healthy view of money. My prayer for you, your family, and your children is from the Psalms:

"Praise the Lord

Blessed are those who fear the Lord, who find great delight in his commands. **Their children will be mighty in the land;** the generation of the upright will be blessed.

Wealth and riches are in their houses, and their righteousness endures forever. Even in darkness light dawns for the upright, for those who are gracious and compassionate and righteous.

Good will come to those who are generous and lend freely, who conduct their affairs with justice. Surely the righteous will never be shaken; they will be remembered forever.

They will have no fear of bad news; their hearts are steadfast, trusting in the Lord. **Their hearts are secure, they will have no fear**; in the end they will look in triumph on their foes.

They have freely scattered their gifts to the poor, their righteousness endures forever; their dignity will be lifted high in honor. The wicked will see and be vexed, they will gnash their teeth and waste away; **the longings of the wicked will come to nothing**" (Psalm 112:1-10 emphasis added).

~~~

The spiritual key which opens the door for you to teach your children about finances is *Knowledge*. Educate yourself so you can do for your children what was never done for you and may your ceiling be their floor! You can do this!

Action Steps

Do you feel insecure teaching your kids about money because you think you don't know enough?

Reading this book is your first step to financial literacy and well done for doing so! The best way to start introducing concepts of money is to buy children's books on the subject which will help you educate your kids about the basics of finance like giving, saving and the impact of debt. Another idea is to find educational videos geared towards kids and finance that you can watch together and have a conversation when the lesson is over. Learn about it with your kids so that your shortcomings do not end up creating financial limitations for them.

When should you open a savings account for your children?

You can open an UTMA or UGMA account (refer to Chapter 4) when they first obtain their social security number after being born. It's an account to deposit birthday checks, holiday checks, cash from jobs like babysitting or checks from jobs such as waiting tables.

At what age should you start teaching your kids to give away a gift they received from Christmas to another family in need?

Every child's emotional development will vary. Most kids fully understand they are helping someone else by giving away an item they own by age 4, and it's up to you if you want to start earlier than that. It's always a good idea to bless another family in need!

At what age should you teach your children to tithe?

When they start working or age 13, whichever happens first. If they are old enough, reward them financially for reading the giving chapter in this book!

How do you send your child on a mission trip?

Your local church is the first place for you to inquire. If they do not have a mission's department, there are mission trip organizations who have built relationships with Church leaders in other countries. They provide local ongoing ministry efforts and take groups for one or two weeks at a time. Do your research on which missions organization you are likely to sign up with if you don't go with your local church and consider going with your kids.

Faith and Finance Make a Great Team

You made it! Congratulations! You read an entire book on the biblical principles of finance and learned practical ways to steward your wealth. I hope you gained clarity about the purpose of money in your life and how to put a financial strategy in place. To help you get started, the below is a list of steps from start to finish:

1. Fully fund an emergency account
2. Open a separate savings account and start your God Fund
3. Interview a financial advisor or certified financial planner
4. Start funding your saving and investing accounts
5. Make a debt pay off plan, if needed
6. Write out a budget, if necessary
7. Purchase the essential insurance products to safeguard your family
8. Research educational videos and children's books about finance to teach your children

The following is a list of scriptures about finances for you to meditate on, memorize, and declare over your life. Doing this will help you begin to discover the biblical truths of money. Faith comes by hearing the word of God so reading it out loud is always a good idea!

"May the Lord increase you a thousand times and bless you as he has promised!" Deuteronomy 1:11

"Some people are always greedy for more, but the godly love to give." Proverbs 21:26

"Good will come to those who are generous and lend freely, who conduct their affairs with justice." Psalm 112:5

"You shall remember the Lord your God, for it is he who gives you power to get wealth, that he may confirm his covenant that he swore to your fathers, as it is this day." Deuteronomy 8:18

"Thus says the Lord, your Redeemer, The Holy One of Israel: I am the Lord your God, Who teaches you to profit, Who leads you by the way you should go." Isaiah 48:17

"The point is this: whoever sows sparingly will also reap sparingly, and whoever sows bountifully will also reap bountifully. Each one must give as he has decided in his heart, not reluctantly or under compulsion, for God loves a cheerful giver. And God is able to make all grace abound to you, so that having all sufficiency in all things at all times, you may abound in every good work." 2 Corinthians 9:6–8

"The Lord will command the blessing on you in your storehouses and in all to which you set your hand, and He will bless you in the land." Deuteronomy 28:8

"Wealth and riches will be in his house, and his righteousness endures forever." Psalm 112:3

"The blessing of the Lord brings wealth, and He adds no sorrow with it." Proverbs 10:22

"Oh, the joys of those who are kind to the poor! The Lord rescues them when they are in trouble." Psalm 41:1

"Bring all the tithes into the storehouse, that there may be food in My house, and try Me now in this, says the Lord of hosts, if I will not open for you the windows of heaven and pour out for you such blessing that there will not be room enough to receive it." Malachi 3:10

"Command those who are rich in this present world not to be arrogant nor to put their hope in wealth, which is so uncertain, but to put their hope in God, who richly provides us with everything for our enjoyment. Command them to do good, to be rich in good deeds, and to be generous and willing to share. In this way they will lay up treasure for themselves as a firm foundation for the coming age, so that they may take hold of the life that is truly life." 1 Timothy 6:17-19

"Honor the Lord with your wealth, with the first fruits of all your crops; then your barns will be filled to overflowing, and your vats will brim over with new wine." Proverbs 3:9

"And my God shall supply all your need according to His riches in glory by Christ Jesus." Philippians 4:19

"I was young and now I am old, yet I have never seen the righteous forsaken or their children begging bread. They are always generous and lend freely; their children will be a blessing." Psalm 37:25-26

"A good person leaves an inheritance for their children's children." Proverbs 13:22a

"No one can serve two masters. Either you will hate the one and love the other, or you will be devoted to the one and despise the other. You cannot serve both God and money." Matthew 6:24

"A generous person will prosper, whoever refreshes others will be refreshed." Proverbs 11:23

"Give, and it will be given to you. A good measure, pressed down, shaken together and running over, will be poured into your lap. For with the measure you use, it will be measured to you." Luke 6:38

"If you belong to Christ, then you are Abraham's seed, and heirs according to the promise." Galatians 3:29

"By humility and the fear of the Lord are riches and honor and life." Proverbs 22:4

References

[1] https://www.oxfordlearnersdictionaries.com/us/definition/english/mindset

[2] https://nonprofitssource.com/online-giving-statistics/church-giving

[3] https://www.irs.gov/charities-non-profits/applying-for-tax-exempt-status

[4] https://www.federalreserve.gov/publications/files/2019-report-economic-well-being-us-households-202005.pdf

[5] https://www.valuepenguin.com/student-loans/average-cost-of-college

[6] https://www.investopedia.com/best-brokers-for-beginners-4587873

[7] https://www.investopedia.com/terms/f/finra.asp

[8] https://smartasset.com/investing/mutual-fund-minimum-investment

[9] https://www.statista.com/statistics/350525/number-etfs-usa/

[10] https://www.sifma.org/wp-content/uploads/2017/08/US-Fact-Book-2018-SIFMA.pdf

[11] https://www.experian.com/blogs/ask-experian/consumer-credit-review/

[12] https://www.experian.com/blogs/ask-experian/consumer-credit-review/

[13] https://www.careercast.com/career-news/11-top-paying-jobs-straight-out-college

[14] https://www.realtor.com/research/march-2020-data/

[15] https://www.nerdwallet.com/blog/finance/budgeting-saving-tools/

[16] https://www.geteducated.com/careers/highest-paying-associate-degree-jobs/

[17] https://www.cdc.gov/nchs/fastats/life-expectancy.htm

[18] https://www.allstate.com/tr/car-insurance/liability-car-insurance-cover.aspx

[19] https://www.iii.org/article/what-umbrella-liability

[20] https://www.healthcare.gov/glossary/health-savings-account-hsa/

[21] http://www.pnhp.org/docs/AJPHBankruptcy2019.pdf

[22] https://www.aaltci.org/long-term-care-insurance/learning-center/long-term-care-statistics.php

[23] https://www.bjs.gov/content/pub/pdf/vit16_sum.pdf

[24] https://www.usnews.com/360-reviews/identity-theft-protection

[25] https://www.valuepenguin.com/average-cost-life-insurance

[26] https://www.investopedia.com/best-online-will-makers-4843732

[27] https://aspe.hhs.gov/poverty-guidelines

[28] https://www.nerdwallet.com/blog/insurance/best-life-insurance-companies/

[29] https://www.nasdaq.com/articles/generational-wealth%3A-why-do-70-of-families-lose-their-wealth-in-the-2nd-generation-2018-10

[30] https://www.merriam-webster.com/dictionary/inheritance

CPSIA information can be obtained
at www.ICGtesting.com
Printed in the USA
BVHW042158190222
629584BV00015B/1357